EMERIL
EVERYDAY

EMERIL
EVERYDAY

It's never been easier to celebrate the goodness of food and make delicious mealtime memories.

CREDITS

©2020 RDA Enthusiast Brands, LLC.
1610 N. 2nd St., Suite 102, Milwaukee WI 53212-3906
All rights reserved.

International Standard Book Number:
978-1-7322161-9-8

Cover Photography:
Emeril Lagasse Portrait: Matt Wagemann
Food: Trusted Studios

Interior Photoraphy, Emeril Lagasse:
Iain Bagwell

Pictured on front cover:
Emeril's Baby Back Ribs, p. 130
Southern-Style Chicken, p. 93
Crispy French Fries, p. 168

Pictured on back cover:
Black Bean, Chorizo & Sweet Potato Chili, p. 54
Clam Sauce, p. 140
Dumpling-Topped Amaretto Cherries, p. 206

Printed in USA
1 3 5 7 9 10 8 6 4 2

CONTENTS

MUST-TRY SIDES, 156

BREAKFAST & BRUNCH, 178

DESSERTS, 202

HAPPY HOME COOKING

There's nothing quite like the joy that comes from cooking a delicious meal for family and friends. Bringing the people you love together over a tasty batch of homemade fried chicken, ooey-gooey mac and cheese and a sensationally sweet cobbler? That's what life is all about.

And I get extra happy making the cooking process easier for you. It's why I've come out with the Pressure Air Fryer. With this single appliance you can do most everything in the kitchen—fast or slow. Want to whip up a spicy batch of chicken wings for your next tailgate party? Cook the wings for a minute using the electric pressure cooker function, then swap lids and give it another 6 minutes with the built-in air fryer.

The combination of pressure cooker and air fryer, slow cooker and air fryer, or even sous vide and air fryer means you'll enjoy meats, sides and desserts that remain tender and moist—with just the right amount of crispiness outside. And you don't need five or more separate appliances to get the job done. Just one. Your Pressure Air Fryer.

So use my latest cookbook—packed with handy tips and advice—to plan and prepare all your family meals. And if you're looking for even more inspiration, join our Emeril Everyday Facebook group today!

PANTRY PERFECT

Preparing incredible foods for family and friends is a surefire way to create invaluable memories. Make the process all the more enjoyable when you have the proper ingredients and tools at the ready.

Try to keep these items on hand to speed up the preparation of all your meals, snacks and even desserts:

All-purpose flour	Dried rosemary	Onion
Bay leaf	Dried thyme	Paprika
Beef broth or beef bouillon	Eggs	Pasta (a variety of dried kinds)
Biscuit/baking mix	Garlic cloves or minced garlic	Pepper
Brown sugar	Garlic powder	Plain dry bread crumbs
Butter	Grated Parmesan cheese	Prepared mustard
Cajun seasoning	Ground allspice	Red wine vinegar
Canola oil	Ground cinnamon	Rice
Cayenne pepper	Ground ginger	Rubbed sage
Chicken broth or chicken bouillon	Ground mustard	Salt
Cider vinegar	Ground nutmeg	Seasoned bread crumbs
Cornstarch	Honey	Soy sauce
Creamy peanut butter	Hot pepper sauce	Stone-ground mustard
Crushed red pepper flakes	Italian seasoning	Sugar
Dijon mustard	Ketchup	Vegetable oil
Dill weed	Lemon juice	White pepper
Dried basil	Lemon-pepper seasoning	White wine
Dried oregano	Mayonnaise	White wine vinegar
Dried parsley flakes	Milk	Worcestershire sauce
	Olive oil	Yellow cornmeal

"Whether you cook occasionally or are at the stove most every night, having a well-equipped kitchen will make the experience that much more enjoyable."

Check the sell-by or use-by dates on pantry items. Throw out any items that are past those dates. Store opened items tightly closed and place in a cool, dry place.

The use-by date on refrigerated items is only for the unopened item. Be sure to keep your fridge's temperature between 34° and 40°.

Store leftovers in covered refrigerator containers or wrap them in plastic wrap or foil; resealable plastic bags also are great for storage.

Store herbs and spices in a kitchen drawer, where you can easily view the contents at a glance. How best to organize? That's up to you. Some people like alphabetizing, while others prefer separating herbs and spices.

THE WELL-STOCKED KITCHEN

Make mealtime easier by stocking up on these foods:

Quick-cooking meats such as boneless chicken, pork tenderloin, pork chops and ground meat make for quick, easy meals. Don't forget sausage, sirloin flank steaks, fish and shrimp. They cook up fast as well.

Pastas and rice mixes are pantry staples that have a long shelf life and complement a multitude of entrees.

Condiments, including ketchup, mustard, mayonnaise, salad dressings, salsa, taco sauce, soy sauce and lemon juice, add flavor without much work.

Fresh produce in the fridge leads to quick side dishes as well as healthy snacks. Ready-to-use salad greens are a modern cook's friend.

Dried herbs, spices, vinegars and seasoning mixes add instant flavor, keep for months and help you prepare an endless number of dishes.

Pasta sauces, olives, beans, broths and canned tomatoes are ideal to have on hand for numerous recipes. You can also use them to create a quick meal.

EQUIVALENT MEASURES

3 TEASPOONS	= 1 tablespoon	**16 TABLESPOONS**	= 1 cup
4 TABLESPOONS	= ¼ cup	**2 CUPS**	= 1 pint
5⅓ TABLESPOONS	= ⅓ cup	**4 CUPS**	= 1 quart
8 TABLESPOONS	= ½ cup	**4 QUARTS**	= 1 gallon

FOOD EQUIVALENTS

MACARONI	1 cup (3½ ounces) uncooked	=	2½ cups cooked
NOODLES, MEDIUM	3 cups (4 ounces) uncooked	=	4 cups cooked
POPCORN	3 cups (4 ounces) uncooked	=	8 cups popped
RICE, LONG GRAIN	1 cup uncooked	=	3 cups cooked
RICE, QUICK-COOKING	1 cup uncooked	=	2 cups cooked
SPAGHETTI	1 cup uncooked	=	4 cups cooked
BREAD	1 slice	=	¾ cup soft crumbs, ¼ cup fine dry crumbs
GRAHAM CRACKERS	7 squares	=	½ cup finely crushed
BUTTERY ROUND CRACKERS	12 crackers	=	½ cup finely crushed
SALTINE CRACKERS	14 crackers	=	½ cup finely crushed

TOOLS OF THE TRADE

Taking a quick inventory of your kitchen gadgets can save a lot of heartache when it comes to dinner prep. Make sure you've got what you need, and let the fun begin!

KITCHEN TOOLS AND GADGETS Having the right tools and gadgets on hand makes every kitchen task easier. Make sure your pantry is equipped vwith these go-to basics.

Apple corer	Pancake turners
Blender and/or	Pastry bag and tips
food processor	Pastry blender
Can and bottle	Pastry brush
opener	Pepper mill
Citrus juicer	Pie server
Citrus zester	Pizza cutter
Colander	Plastic mixing
Cookie cutters	spoons
Corkscrew	Potato masher
Cutting boards,	Rolling pin
wood and plastic	Slotted spoons,
Dough cutter/scraper	large and small
Egg separator	Spatulas, rubber
Egg slicer	and metal
Garlic press	Storage and freezer
Hand grater/shredder	containers
Ladles, large	Thermometers:
and small	Instant-read,
Measuring cups,	candy/deep-fry,
dry and liquid	meat, oven,
Measuring spoons	refrigerator/
Meat fork	freezer
Meat mallet/	Timer
tenderizer	Tongs
Metal skewers	Vegetable peeler
Metal strainer	Wire racks
or sieve	Wire whisks in
Mixers, stand	assorted sizes
or hand	Wooden mixing
Mixing bowls	spoons

KITCHEN CUTLERY A basic set of knives is essential to any kitchen. There are a variety of knives made from numerous materials. The best knives, made from high-carbon steel, are resistant to corrosion (unlike carbon steel) and remain sharper longer than stainless steel.

Utility Knife This 6-in. knife is the right size to slice small foods.

Carving Knife This 8- to 10-in. knife is perfect for slicing roasts and turkey.

Chef's Knife This multipurpose knife with an 8-to 10-in. blade is used for mincing, chopping and dicing.

Paring Knife This 3- to 4-in. knife is used for peeling, mincing and slicing small foods.

Serrated or Bread Knife This knife's serrated blade is used for slicing breads, cakes and delicate foods. An 8-in. knife is most versatile, but many lengths are available.

Santoku This is a Japanese variation of a chef's knife. The 6½- to 7-in. multipurpose knife is used for mincing, chopping, dicing and slicing. The dimple design of the blade helps reduce drag during slicing.

Boning Knife- This knife's 5- or 6-in. tapered blade is designed to remove the meat from poultry, beef, pork or fish bones.

Kitchen Shears This versatile tool is used to snip fresh herbs, disjoint chicken, trim pastry, cut kitchen string, and perform many other tasks.

Steel This long, thin rod with a handle is used to smooth out small rough spots on the edge of a knife blade and to reset the edge of the blade. You can also use a whetstone or electric knife sharpener to sharpen knives.

For the best cooking and baking results, ingredients need to be measured accurately with the correct measuring tool. Every cook needs the right measuring cups, as well as a good set of measuring spoons.

Liquid Measuring Cups are mostly available in either clear glass or plastic. They usually have a pouring spout and come in 1-cup, 2-cup, 4-cup and 8-cup sizes. Use liquid measuring cups for pourable ingredients such as milk, water, oil, honey, molasses and corn syrup.

Dry Measuring Cups are found in metal or plastic. They're designed with an even rim for leveling off ingredients. These cups come in sets of ¼ cup, ⅓ cup, ½ cup and 1 cup, and some sets may also include ⅛ cup, ⅔ cup or ¾ cup. Use these cups for measuring dry ingredients or those that mound, such as brown sugar, flour, nuts, chocolate chips, sour cream and shortening.

Measuring Spoons are usually made of metal or plastic and feature even rims. A standard set includes ¼ teaspoon, ½ teaspoon, 1 teaspoon and 1 tablespoon. Some also have ⅛ teaspoon, ¾ teaspoon or ½ tablespoon measures. Use them for liquid and dry ingredients.

Liquid Ingredients. Place the measuring cup on a flat surface and view at eye level for a standard liquid measure (some measuring cups allow for viewing from above). For easier pouring and cleanup, spray the cup with cooking spray before adding sticky ingredients such as honey, molasses, corn syrup or peanut butter.

Sour Cream and Yogurt. Spoon sour cream or yogurt into a dry measuring cup, allowing the mixture to mound a little. Level by sweeping a straight-edged spatula or knife across the top of the cup.

Dry Ingredients. Level any ingredient measured in a dry measuring cup by sweeping a straight-edged spatula or knife across the top.

Powdery or Fine-Textured Ingredients. Gently spoon dry ingredients, such as sugar or cornmeal, into a dry measuring cup over the canister. Allow the ingredient to overflow, then level the top. Stir or "fluff" flour to aerate it before spooning it into the cup.

Dry Bulk Ingredients. Spoon bulk ingredients, like nuts or chips, into the cup, then level the top.

Brown Sugar. Because of brown sugar's moist texture, most recipes call for it to be packed into a measuring cup for an accurate measurement. Press brown sugar into a cup using your fingers or the back of a spoon, then level the top.

Shortening. Press shortening from a can into dry measuring cups with a spatula to ensure that it is solidly packed without air bubbles, then level the top.

Stick Butter, Margarine or Shortening. The wrappers for these products come with markings for tablespoons, ¼ cup, ⅓ cup and ½ cup. Use a knife to cut the desired amount.

Measuring Spoons. Measure dry ingredients, such as flour, sugar or spices, by heaping them into the spoon, then leveling the top. Pour liquid ingredients into a measuring spoon over a sink, or a custard cup or small bowl, if you want to catch spills.

POWER UP

with Your Emeril Lagasse Pressure Air Fryer

Today's families are turning to this all-in-one cooker
for everything from appetizers to desserts. Review these tips
to save time—and serve sensational meals every day.

PRESSURE AIR FRYER 101

Before you get cooking with your Pressure Air Fryer, keep these basics in mind.

Do Your Homework.

Make sure to thoroughly review the instruction manual that came with your Pressure Air Fryer before you start cooking. Understand the various aspects of the machine, and you'll have no trouble following the recipes in this cookbook.

Understand What's What.

Your device comes with a lid for pressure-cooking and a separate lid for air-frying. Take a moment to familiarize yourself with each. Similarly, check any additional accessories, such as the wire racks, mesh basket or glass lid to be sure nothing was damaged during shipping.

Give It Some Space.

Place your Pressure Air Fryer on a clean, flat surface. When operating the unit, be sure to leave at least 5 inches of free space on the back and sides, and above the device. Never put the Pressure Air Fryer on a stovetop surface.

Collect that Condensation.

Before you cook anything, make sure the condensation collector is firmly attached to the unit. Remember to remove the collector and wash it with warm, soapy water regularly.

Keep It Clean.

Remove the inner lid of the pressure cooker lid and clean it after every use. Gently pull off the inner lid outer gasket and wash it with warm, soapy water. Check that the gasket is clean, flexible and not torn before each use.

The Temperature is Key.

The Pressure Air Fryer offers numerous temperature settings. These setting are based on temperature and not necessarily on the ingredients. For instance, the recipe for *Crab Quiche Bites (p. 185)* relies on the temperature obtained via the poultry setting. *Dumpling-Topped Amaretto Cherries (p. 206)* simmer best at the vegetables setting. Select the settings noted in the recipe, even when they don't seem to align with the items you're cooking.

Learn how to release the pressure safely when cooking with the Pressure Air Fryer. Because the escaping steam is hot enough to burn you, it's imperative you read and understand the directions that came with your unit.

Generally speaking, the pressure cooker function relies on two methods to release steam: natural release and rapid or quick release. Natural release occurs when the device cools down and releases pressure naturally. This method is ideal for meats, foods that increase in volume as they cook, and dishes that are largely liquid, like soups.

Quick release occurs when you slide the steam release switch to the open position and quickly let it go. This releases a burst of extremely hot steam from the unit. Quick-release pressure when preparing eggs, vegetables and other delicate ingredients. Avoid this method when cooking liquid foods like soups; the liquid can boil up and vent through the pressure release valve.

> * *Storage tip: Don't lose the power cord! Simply stash it inside the pot for safekeeping.*

AIR-FRY WITH EASE

One the most popular functions of the Emeril Lagasse Pressure Air Fryer is its ability to crisp up foods without deep frying. When using the air fryer option, remember these tips.

Snack Attack

Snacks that are traditionally baked in the oven can most often be prepared using the appliance's air fry function. Small, bite-sized snacks usually require a shorter cooking time than larger appetizers.

Oil Alert

When using the air fry function, add the amount of oil called for in a recipe or spritz foods with oil before cooking. Never use the device to deep-fry foods.

Put a Lid on It

The air fry preset will not function unless the wire harnesses are aligned properly. To attach the air fryer lid, place the lid on top of the base, aligning the pins in the lid's wire harness with the holes in the base's wire harness. Do not twist the air fryer lid to close.

SNACKS & APPETIZERS

Let's get this party started! Select your favorite playlist to set the mood, then treat your guests to apps and beverages they'll still be talking about long after the party's over.

AIR-FRYER PICKLES

PREP: 20 MIN. + STANDING | **AIR-FRY:** 15 MIN./BATCH | **MAKES:** 32 SLICES

32 dill pickle slices

½ cup all-purpose flour

½ tsp. salt

3 large eggs, lightly beaten

2 Tbsp. dill pickle juice

½ tsp. cayenne pepper

½ tsp. garlic powder

2 cups panko bread crumbs

2 Tbsp. minced fresh cilantro

Olive oil cooking spray

Ranch salad dressing, optional

1. Let pickles stand on a paper towel until liquid is almost absorbed, about 15 minutes.

2. Meanwhile, in a shallow bowl, combine flour and salt. In another shallow bowl, whisk eggs, pickle juice, cayenne and garlic powder. Combine panko and cilantro in a third shallow bowl. Dip pickles in flour mixture to coat both sides; shake off excess. Dip in egg mixture, then in crumb mixture, patting to help coating adhere. Spritz pickles with olive oil spray.

3. Place tall wire rack into inner pot. Arrange pickles in a single layer on rack. Close air frying lid. Press air fry function; select custom setting. Press timer; set to 7 minutes. Start.

4. Turn pickles over and spritz with olive oil spray. Air-fry an additional 7-10 minutes or until golden brown and crispy. Repeat with remaining pickles. Serve immediately. If desired, serve with ranch dressing.

1 PICKLE SLICE: *26 cal., 1g fat (0 sat. fat), 13mg chol., 115mg sod., 4g carb. (0 sugars, 0 fiber), 1g pro.*

How Many Appetizers Should You Prepare?

For cocktails before dinner, plan on 3-4 different types of apps at 4-5 pieces per person. This way, no one is too full to enjoy the meal you've prepared.

For an open house buffet, you'll need 4-5 types of appetizers and 4-6 pieces per person. Be sure to have a solid combination of flavors and textures.

For a light dinner of finger foods, consider 6-8 appetizers and roughly 14-16 pieces per guest. Keep extras at the ready for fast and easy restocking.

MOROCCAN PHYLLO BUNDLES

PREP: 30 MIN. | **SAUTE:** 15 MIN. | **AIR-FRY:** 10 MIN./BATCH
MAKES: 28 APPETIZERS (1 CUP SAUCE)

½ lb. ground beef

½ small onion, finely chopped

3 Tbsp. dried currants

¼ tsp. salt

¼ tsp. ground cumin

⅛ tsp. ground cinnamon

⅛ tsp. ground nutmeg

Dash cayenne pepper

⅛ tsp. pepper

2 tsp. cornstarch

¼ cup water

14 sheets phyllo dough (14x9 in.)

¼ cup butter, melted

SPICY MANGO SAUCE

¾ cup plain yogurt

½ cup chopped peeled mango

¼ tsp. salt

¼ tsp. ground cumin

¼ tsp. cayenne pepper

1 tsp. dried currants

1. Press saute function; select beef setting. Cook the beef and onion until meat is no longer pink, breaking into crumbles; drain. Stir in currants and seasonings. Combine cornstarch and water until smooth; gradually stir into beef mixture. Bring to a boil; cook and stir for 2 minutes or until thickened. Press cancel; remove inner pot from the heat.

2. Place 1 sheet of phyllo dough on a work surface with a short end facing you; brush with melted butter. Place another sheet of phyllo on top and brush with butter. (Keep remaining phyllo covered with a damp towel to prevent it from drying out.) Cut the 2 layered sheets into four 14x2¼-in. strips.

3. Place a rounded teaspoonful of filling on lower corner of each strip. Fold dough over filling, forming a triangle. Fold triangle up, then fold triangle over, forming another triangle. Continue folding, like a flag, until you come to the end of the strip. Brush end of dough with butter; press onto triangle to seal. Turn triangle and brush top with butter. Repeat with remaining phyllo and filling. Wipe inner pot clean.

4. Place tall wire rack into inner pot. Arrange triangles in a single layer on rack. Cover with air frying lid. Press air fry function; select bake setting. Press timer; set to 5 minutes. Start.

5. Turn triangles over and air-fry an additional 2 minutes or until lightly browned. Repeat with remaining triangles.

6. For sauce, in a food processor or blender, combine yogurt, mango, salt, cumin and cayenne. Pulse until mango is slightly broken down. Stir in currants. Serve with warm appetizers.

1 TRIANGLE WITH 1½ TSP. SAUCE: *70 cal., 3g fat (2g sat. fat), 10mg chol., 108mg sod., 8g carb. (2g sugars, 0 fiber), 3g pro.*

BACON CHEDDAR POTATO SKINS

PREP: 10 MIN. | **PRESSURE-COOK:** 12 MIN. | **AIR-FRY:** 10 MIN./BATCH | **MAKES:** 8 SERVINGS

4 medium baking potatoes

3 Tbsp. canola oil

½ tsp. salt

¼ tsp. garlic powder

¼ tsp. paprika

⅛ tsp. pepper

1 Tbsp. grated Parmesan cheese

8 bacon strips, cooked and crumbled

1½ cups shredded cheddar cheese

½ cup sour cream

4 green onions, sliced

1. Place tall wire rack and 1 cup water into inner pot. Scrub potatoes under running water; pierce multiple times with a fork and set on wire rack. Lock pressure lid. Press pressure function; select vegetables setting. Set to long cook time (12 minutes). Start.

2. Quick-release pressure. Remove potatoes and wire rack; discard cooking juices. Wipe insert clean.

3. When cool enough to handle, cut potatoes in half lengthwise; scoop out pulp, leaving a ¼-in. shell (save pulp for another use). Combine oil, salt, garlic powder, paprika and pepper; brush over both sides of skins. Sprinkle with Parmesan cheese.

4. Place tall wire rack into inner pot. Arrange potatoes, skin side down, in a single layer on rack. Close air frying lid. Press air fry function; select custom setting. Press timer; set to 7 minutes. Start.

5. Sprinkle shells with bacon and cheddar cheese. Air-fry an additional 2 minutes or until cheese is melted. Repeat with remaining potato skins. Serve immediately with sour cream and green onions.

1 POTATO SKIN: *350 cal., 19g fat (7g sat. fat), 33mg chol., 460mg sod., 34g carb. (2g sugars, 4g fiber), 12g pro.*

APPLE CIDER

PREP: 5 MIN. | **SLOW-COOK:** 2 HOURS | **MAKES:** ABOUT 2 QT.

8	whole cloves
8	cups apple cider or juice
½	cup water
1	cinnamon stick (3 in.)
1	tea bag

1. Place cloves on a double thickness of cheesecloth; bring up corners of cloth and tie with kitchen string to form a bag. Place the remaining ingredients into inner pot; add spice bag.

2. Cover with glass lid. Press slow cook function; select vegetables setting. Set to medium cook time (2 hours). Start.

3. Discard spice bag, cinnamon stick and tea bag before serving.

1 CUP: *120 cal., 0 fat (0 sat. fat), 0 chol., 25mg sod., 30g carb. (26g sugars, 0 fiber), 0 pro.*

Making a Spice Bag

1. Use a spice bag to contain spices, citrus peel, bay leaves or other items. Place seasonings on a double thickness of cheesecloth. Bring up edges and tie securely with kitchen string.

2. If you prefer, you can use a cloth tea sachet (available in tea shops) instead of creating a cheesecloth spice bag. Discard contents of the spice bag or sachet after using.

PUMPKIN FRIES WITH CHIPOTLE-MAPLE SAUCE

PREP: 25 MIN. | **AIR-FRY:** 6 MIN./BATCH | **MAKES:** 4 SERVINGS

½ cup plain Greek yogurt

2 Tbsp. maple syrup

2 to 3 tsp. minced chipotle peppers in adobo sauce

⅛ tsp. plus ½ tsp. salt, divided

1 medium pie pumpkin

¼ tsp. garlic powder

¼ tsp. ground cumin

¼ tsp. chili powder

¼ tsp. pepper

1. In a small bowl, combine yogurt, maple syrup, chipotle peppers and ⅛ tsp. salt. Refrigerate, covered, until serving.

2. Peel pumpkin; cut in half lengthwise; discard seeds or save for toasting. Cut into ½-in. strips. Transfer to a large bowl. Sprinkle with remaining ½ tsp. salt, garlic powder, cumin, chili powder and pepper; toss to coat.

3. Place tall wire rack into inner pot. Arrange pumpkin in a single layer on greased rack. Close air frying lid. Press air fry function; select vegetables setting. Press temp setting; set to 400°. Press timer; set to 6 minutes. Start. Turn pumpkin over. Air fry an additional 3 minutes or until browned and crisp. Repeat with remaining pumpkin. Serve with sauce.

½ CUP FRIES WITH 2 TBSP. SAUCE: *151 cal., 3g fat (2g sat. fat), 8mg chol., 413mg sod., 31g carb. (12g sugars, 2g fiber), 5g pro.*

* *To create a sweet and spicy dip, mix ½ cup mayonnaise with 2 tablespoons cherry preserves and 4 teaspoons prepared horseradish. This is great on roast beef sandwiches, too.*

WASABI CRAB CAKES

PREP: 20 MIN. | **AIR-FRY:** 10 MIN./BATCH | **MAKES:** 2 DOZEN (½ CUP SAUCE)

1 medium sweet red pepper, finely chopped

1 celery rib, finely chopped

3 green onions, finely chopped

2 large egg whites

3 Tbsp. mayonnaise

¼ tsp. prepared wasabi

¼ tsp. salt

⅓ cup plus ½ cup dry bread crumbs, divided

1½ cups lump crabmeat, drained

Olive oil cooking spray

SAUCE

1 celery rib, chopped

⅓ cup mayonnaise

1 green onion, chopped

1 Tbsp. finely chopped cornichons

½ tsp. prepared wasabi

¼ tsp. celery salt

1. In a small bowl, combine the first 7 ingredients; stir in ⅓ cup bread crumbs. Gently fold in crab.

2. Place remaining bread crumbs in a shallow bowl. Drop heaping tablespoonfuls of crab mixture into crumbs. Gently coat and shape into ¾-in.-thick patties. Cover tall wire rack with foil. Coat foil with cooking spray. Place tall wire rack into inner pot. Arrange crab cakes into a single layer on foil. Close air frying lid. Press air fry function; select custom setting. Press timer; set to 5 minutes. Start.

3. Turn crab cakes over and spritz with additional cooking spray. Air-fry an additional 5 minutes or until lightly browned. Repeat with remaining crab cakes.

4. Meanwhile, place sauce ingredients in food processor; pulse 2-3 times to blend or until desired consistency is reached. Serve crab cakes immediately with dipping sauce.

1 CRAB CAKE WITH 1 TSP. SAUCE: *62 cal., 4g fat (1g sat. fat), 12mg chol., 168mg sod., 3g carb. (1g sugars, 0 fiber), 3g pro.*

"Spice is life. ... Yes, food is serious, but you should have fun with it."

SPICY CHICKEN WINGS WITH BLUE CHEESE DIP

PREP: 25 MIN. | **PRESSURE-COOK:** 1 MIN. + RELEASING | **AIR-FRY:** 6 MIN./BATCH
MAKES: 2 DOZEN (1¾ CUPS DIP)

1 cup soy sauce

⅔ cup sugar

2 garlic cloves, minced

2 tsp. salt

2 tsp. grated orange zest

½ tsp. coarsely ground pepper

3 lbs. (total) chicken wingettes and drumettes

3 tsp. chili powder

¾ tsp. cayenne pepper

¾ tsp. hot pepper sauce

BLUE CHEESE DIP

1 cup mayonnaise

½ cup crumbled blue cheese

⅓ cup buttermilk

½ tsp. coarsely ground pepper

1. In a small bowl, combine the soy sauce, sugar, garlic, salt, orange zest and pepper; divide in half. Add chicken pieces to inner pot. Top with half the sauce and toss to coat. Lock pressure lid. Press pressure function; select poultry setting. Press timer; set to 1 minute. Start.

2. Let pressure release naturally for 10 minutes; quick-release any remaining pressure.

3. Remove chicken from inner pot with a slotted spoon to a large bowl. In a small bowl, combine chili powder, cayenne and remaining sauce mixture. Drizzle over chicken. Discard cooking juices in inner pot and wipe clean.

4. Place tall wire rack into inner pot. Arrange chicken in a single layer on rack. Close air frying lid. Press air fry function; select poultry setting. Press temp; set to 400°. Press timer; set to 6 min. Cook chicken in batches, adding more time as necessary for wings to reach 170°. In a small bowl, whisk dip ingredients. Serve with wings.

1 PIECE WITH ABOUT 1 TBSP. DIP: *182 cal., 12g fat (3g sat. fat), 43mg chol., 1096mg sod., 6g carb. (6g sugars, 0 fiber), 12g pro.*

Make Your Own Wingettes

1. Place chicken wing on a cutting board. With a sharp knife, cut between the joint at the top of the tip end. Discard the tips or use for making broth.

2. Take the remaining wing and cut between the joints. Proceed with the recipe as directed.

CHAI TEA

PREP: 15 MIN. | **SLOW-COOK:** 8 HOURS | **MAKES:** 12 SERVINGS (3 QT.)

15 slices fresh gingerroot
(about 3 oz.)

3 cinnamon sticks (3 in.)

25 whole cloves

15 cardamom pods,
lightly crushed

3 whole peppercorns

3½ qt. water

8 black tea bags

1 can (14 oz.) sweetened
condensed milk

1. Place first 5 ingredients on a double thickness of cheesecloth. Gather corners of cloth to enclose spices; tie securely with string. Place spice bag and water into inner pot. Cover with glass lid. Press slow cook function; select pork setting. Set to medium cook time (8 hours). Start.

2. Discard spice bag. Add tea bags; steep, covered, 3-5 minutes according to taste. Discard tea bags. Stir in milk; heat through. Serve warm.

1 CUP: *109 cal., 3g fat (2g sat. fat), 11mg chol., 50mg sod., 19g carb. (18g sugars, 0 fiber), 3g pro.*

"I can't tell you enough about cinnamon. Cinnamon is an awesome spice."

SWEET & SPICY ASIAN MEATBALLS

PREP: 25 MIN. | **AIR-FRY:** 10 MIN./BATCH | **SLOW-COOK:** 2 HOURS
MAKES: ABOUT 4½ DOZEN

1 large egg, lightly beaten

½ medium onion, finely chopped

⅓ cup sliced water chestnuts, finely chopped

3 Tbsp. minced fresh cilantro

1 jalapeño pepper, seeded and finely chopped

3 Tbsp. soy sauce

4 garlic cloves, minced

1 Tbsp. minced fresh gingerroot

⅔ cup panko bread crumbs

2 lbs. ground pork

SAUCE

½ cup hoisin sauce

⅓ cup soy sauce

¼ cup shaoxing rice wine or pale dry sherry

3 Tbsp. brown sugar

3 Tbsp. honey

2 Tbsp. fresh lime juice

2 Tbsp. Vietnamese chili garlic sauce (tuong ot toi)

3 garlic cloves, minced

1 Tbsp. Emeril's® Cajun Seasoning Blend

1 Tbsp. minced fresh gingerroot

1 Tbsp. toasted sesame oil

½ tsp. Chinese five-spice powder

Thinly sliced green onions and toasted sesame seeds, optional

1. In a large bowl, combine the first 8 ingredients; stir in bread crumbs. Add pork; mix lightly but thoroughly. Shape into 1½-in. balls. Arrange meatballs into single layers on greased stacked wire racks. Close air frying lid. Press air fry function; select custom setting. Press timer; set to 10 minutes. Start. Cook in batches until lightly browned.

2. Meanwhile, in a small bowl, mix sauce ingredients. Remove stacked wire racks. Return all meatballs to inner pot. Pour sauce over browned meatballs. Cover with glass lid. Press slow cook function, select pork setting. Press timer; set to 2 hours. Start.

3. Transfer to serving platter and, if desired, sprinkle with green onions and sesame seeds.

1 MEATBALL: *62 cal., 3g fat (1g sat. fat), 15mg chol., 198mg sod., 4g carb. (3g sugars, 0 fiber), 4g pro.*

CHIPOTLE CARNE GUISADA NACHOS

PREP: 20 MIN. | **SLOW-COOK:** 5 HOURS | **AIR-FRY:** 5 MIN. | **MAKES:** 8 SERVINGS

1   can (8 oz.) tomato sauce

2   chopped chipotle peppers in adobo sauce plus 2 Tbsp. sauce

12 garlic cloves, minced

1   Tbsp. chili powder

1½ tsp. ground cumin

¼   tsp. salt

½   tsp. pepper

¾   cup beef stock

2½ lbs. beef stew meat

10 cups (about 8 oz.) tortilla chips

4   cups shredded Mexican cheese blend

Optional toppings: Chopped tomatoes, sliced green onions, chopped cilantro and sour cream

1. Combine the first 9 ingredients in the inner pot. Cover with glass lid. Press slow cook function; select beef setting. Press timer; set to 5 hours. Start.

2. Remove beef; shred with 2 forks. Reserve 1 cup cooking juices; discard remaining juices. Skim fat from reserved juices. Return beef and reserved juices to inner pot. Layer half of the tortilla chips and cheese over beef; repeat layers.

3. Cover with air frying lid. Press air fry function; select custom setting. Press timer; set to 5 minutes. Start.

4. Remove chips and beef from inner pot to serving platter. Add optional toppings if desired.

½ CUP: *606 cal., 36g fat (14g sat. fat), 138mg chol., 888mg sod., 27g carb. (1g sugars, 2g fiber), 43g pro.*

Chipotle peppers are a quick, easy way to add excitement to dishes. Often found canned in a chili sauce, chipotles are medium to hot in spice levels so they work well in a variety of dishes...and with a variety of palates!

PEPPER POPPERS

PREP: 20 MIN. | **AIR-FRY:** 15 MIN./BATCH | **MAKES:** ABOUT 2 DOZEN

- 1 pkg. (8 oz.) cream cheese, softened
- ¾ cup shredded cheddar cheese
- ¾ cup shredded Monterey Jack cheese
- 6 bacon strips, cooked and crumbled
- ¼ tsp. salt
- ¼ tsp. garlic powder
- ¼ tsp. chili powder
- ¼ tsp. smoked paprika
- 1 lb. fresh jalapeños, halved lengthwise and seeded
- ½ cup dry bread crumbs
  Olive oil cooking spray
  French onion dip or sour cream, optional

1. In a large bowl, combine the cheeses, bacon and seasonings; mix well. Spoon 1½-2 tablespoonfuls into each pepper half. Roll in bread crumbs.

2. Cover tall wire rack with foil. Coat foil with olive oil cooking spray. Place tall wire rack into inner pot. Arrange peppers into a single layer on foil. Close air frying lid. Press air fry function; select custom setting. Press timer; set to 15 minutes for spicy flavor, 20 minutes for medium and 25 minutes for mild, being careful not to overcook. Start. Repeat with remaining peppers. If desired, serve with dip or sour cream.

1 STUFFED PEPPER HALF: *81 cal., 6g fat (4g sat. fat), 18mg chol., 145mg sod., 3g carb. (1g sugars, 1g fiber), 3g pro.*

SOUPS, STEWS & SANDWICHES

It's true. Simple preparation, easy cooking methods and a handful of quality ingredients lead to sensational foods. And nothing proves that more than the comforting classics assembled here.

SAUSAGE & CHICKEN GUMBO

PREP: 55 MIN. | **SLOW-COOK:** 8 HOURS | **MAKES:** 6 SERVINGS

¼ cup all-purpose flour

¼ cup canola oil

4 cups chicken broth, divided

1 pkg. (14 oz.) smoked sausage, cut into ½-in. slices

1 cup frozen sliced okra, thawed

1 small green pepper, chopped

1 medium onion, chopped

1 celery rib, chopped

3 garlic cloves, minced

½ tsp. pepper

¼ tsp. salt

¼ tsp. cayenne pepper

2 cups coarsely shredded cooked chicken

1 Tbsp. gumbo filé powder, optional

Hot cooked rice

1. Press saute function; select beef setting. Press timer; set to 1 hour. Mix flour and oil in inner pot. Cook and stir until dark reddish brown, about 45 minutes. Gradually whisk in 3 cups broth. Press cancel.

2. Stir in sausage, vegetables, garlic and seasonings. Cover with glass lid. Press slow cook function; select pork setting. Set to medium cook time (8 hours). Start.

3. Stir in chicken, remaining broth and, if desired, filé powder; heat through. Serve with rice.

1 CUP: *427 cal., 31g fat (9g sat. fat), 89mg chol., 1551mg sod., 11g carb. (4g sugars, 1g fiber), 25g pro.*

"A great bowl of gumbo is satisfying and comforting on even the gloomiest of days."

THAI BUTTERNUT SQUASH SOUP

PREP: 40 MIN. | **SAUTE:** 20 MIN. | **CANNING:** 1 HOUR | **MAKES:** 4 PINT JARS

5	cups cubed peeled butternut squash (½-in. cubes)
2½	cups chicken broth
1	medium sweet red pepper, chopped
2	shallots, finely chopped
4	garlic cloves, minced
1	Tbsp. minced fresh gingerroot
1	serrano pepper, seeded and finely chopped
2	Tbsp. lime juice
1	Tbsp. honey
1½	tsp. salt
1	tsp. grated lime zest
¼	tsp. cayenne pepper
	Optional: Coconut milk, sliced red onion, cilantro and lime wedges

1. Combine all ingredients in inner pot; cover with glass lid. Press saute function; select vegetables setting. Press timer; set to 20 minutes. Start. Cook until squash is tender.

2. Cool slightly. Process soup in batches in blender or food processor. Ladle warm soup into 4 hot 1-pint canning jars, leaving 1-in. headspace. Remove air bubbles and adjust headspace, if necessary, by adding more warm soup. Wipe rims. Center lids on jars; screw on bands until a little more than fingertip tight. Wipe inner pot clean.

3. Place wire rack with handles into inner pot. Arrange jars on rack. Carefully pour hot water into inner pot until water level reaches a quarter of the way up sides of jars. Lock pressure lid. Press canning function. Press timer; set to 60 minutes. Start.

4. Quick-release pressure; remove pressure lid. Let stand 5 minutes before removing from unit to cool further. When jars are completely cool, lids should be tightly sealed to jars. When center of lid is pressed, there shouldn't be any give or springing motion. If lid springs or gives when pushed, the canning process was not successful and food must be reprocessed immediately or refrigerated and used within 5 days.

5. If desired, serve hot soup with coconut milk, red onion, cilantro and lime wedges.

1 CUP: *77 cal., 0 fat (0 sat. fat), 2mg chol., 756mg sod., 19g carb. (6g sugars, 3g fiber), 2g pro.*

✳ | *If the screw bands are too loose, liquid may escape from jars during processing and the seals may fail. If the screw bands are too tight, air cannot vent during processing and food will discolor during storage. Overtightening also may cause lids to buckle and jars to break. Do not use above 2,000 feet above sea level.*

GREEN TOMATO BLT

PREP: 20 MIN. | **AIR-FRY:** 11 MIN./BATCH | **MAKES:** 4 SERVINGS

2 medium green tomatoes (about 10 oz.)

½ tsp. salt

¼ tsp. pepper

1 large egg, beaten

¼ cup all-purpose flour

1 cup panko bread crumbs

Olive oil spray

½ cup mayonnaise

2 green onions, finely chopped

1 tsp. chopped fresh basil

8 slices whole wheat bread, toasted

8 cooked center-cut bacon strips

4 Bibb or Boston lettuce leaves

1. Cut tomato into 8 slices, about ¼ in. thick each. Sprinkle tomato slices with salt and pepper. Place egg, flour and bread crumbs in separate shallow bowls. Dip tomato slices in flour, shaking off excess, then dip into egg, and finally into bread crumb mixture, patting to help adhere.

2. Place tall wire rack into inner pot. Arrange slices in a single layer on rack. Spritz with olive oil spray. Cover with air frying lid; select custom setting. Press timer; set to 6 minutes. Start.

3. Turn tomatoes over. Air-fry 5-7 minutes longer or until lightly browned. Repeat with remaining tomato slices.

4. Meanwhile, mix mayonnaise, green onions and basil. Layer each of 4 slices of bread with 2 bacon strips, 1 lettuce leaf and 2 tomato slices. Spread mayonnaise mixture over remaining slices of bread; place over top. Serve immediately.

1 SANDWICH: *472 cal., 27g fat (5g sat. fat), 37mg chol., 956mg sod., 42g carb. (6g sugars, 5g fiber), 16g pro.*

Add a Little Pizazz to Your Sandwich

Mayo with a Kick
Mix ⅓ cup mayonnaise with ⅓-½ tsp. prepared horseradish, ½ tsp. minced chives and ¼-½ tsp. garlic powder.

Blazing Mustard
Combine ½ cup ground mustard, 1½ tsp. sugar and ½ tsp. salt. Stir in 3 Tbsp. water and 2 Tbsp. white vinegar until smooth.

Artichoke Pepperoncini Sandwich Spread
Process ⅓ cup rinsed and drained water-packed artichoke hearts with 2 whole pepperoncini peppers in a food processor.

FRENCH ONION SOUP

PREP: 10 MIN. | **SAUTE:** 30 MIN. | **PRESSURE-COOK:** 12 MIN. | **AIR-FRY:** 2 MIN.
MAKES: 6 SERVINGS

¼ cup butter

4 cups thinly sliced onions

6 cups beef broth

1 garlic clove, minced

1 tsp. minced fresh thyme

1 tsp. Worcestershire sauce

½ tsp. salt

2 Tbsp. brandy, optional

6 slices French bread
   (¾ in. thick), buttered
   and toasted

6 slices Swiss cheese

1. Press saute function; select vegetables setting. Press timer; set to 30 minutes. Start. Melt butter in inner pot. Add onions; cook and stir until tender and golden, 25-30 minutes. Press cancel.

2. Stir in broth, garlic, thyme, Worcestershire sauce and salt. Lock pressure lid. Press pressure function; select vegetables setting. Set to long cook time (12 minutes). Start.

3. Quick-release pressure. If desired, stir in brandy. Ladle soup into individual serving crocks. Place tall wire rack into inner pot. Arrange buttered toast on rack. Top with cheese. Cover with air frying lid. Press air fry function; select custom setting. Press timer; set to 2 minutes. Start. Cook until cheese is melted. Serve toasts over soup.

1 SERVING: *188 cal., 11g fat (7g sat. fat), 30mg chol., 398mg sod., 17g carb. (3g sugars, 2g fiber), 6g pro.*

*"I can sleep better at night if
I can improve an individual's
knowledge about food and wine,
and do it on a daily basis."*

CHEESY HAM & CORN CHOWDER

PREP: 20 MIN. | **SLOW-COOK:** 10 HOURS 25 MIN. | **MAKES:** 12 SERVINGS (3¾ QT.)

1½ lbs. russet potatoes
(about 3 medium), peeled
and cut into ½-in. cubes

4 cups fresh or frozen corn,
thawed (about 20 oz.)

4 cups cubed ham

2 small onions, chopped

4 celery ribs, chopped

4 garlic cloves, minced

¼ tsp. pepper

3 cups chicken broth

2 Tbsp. cornstarch

2 cups whole milk

2 cups shredded sharp
cheddar cheese

1 cup sour cream

3 Tbsp. minced fresh
parsley

1. Combine the first 8 ingredients in inner pot. Cover with glass lid. Press slow cook function; select vegetables setting. Select timer; set to 10 hours. Start. Cook until potatoes are tender.

2. In a small bowl, mix cornstarch and milk until smooth; stir into soup. Cover with glass lid. Press slow cook function; select vegetables setting. Press timer; set to 25 minutes. Press temp; set to 212°. Start. Cook until thickened, stirring occasionally. Stir in cheese, sour cream and parsley until cheese is melted.

1¼ CUPS: *291 cal., 14g fat (7g sat. fat), 56mg chol., 976mg sod., 23g carb. (7g sugars, 2g fiber), 19g pro.*

✳ *To keep the potatoes from browning, as you cut them, place them in a container of water; drain before adding to the pot.*

BLACK BEAN, CHORIZO & SWEET POTATO CHILI

PREP: 10 MIN. | **SAUTE:** 15 MIN. | **SLOW-COOK:** 6 HOURS | **MAKES:** 16 SERVINGS (4 QT.)

1   lb. fresh chorizo,
    casings removed

1   large onion, chopped

2   poblano peppers,
    finely chopped

2   jalapeño peppers, seeded
    and finely chopped

3   Tbsp. tomato paste

3   large sweet potatoes,
    peeled and cut into
    ½-in. cubes

4   cans (14½ oz. each)
    fire-roasted diced
    tomatoes, undrained

2   cans (15 oz. each) black
    beans, rinsed and drained

2   cups beef stock

2   Tbsp. chili powder

1   Tbsp. dried oregano

1   Tbsp. ground coriander

1   Tbsp. ground cumin

1   Tbsp. smoked paprika

¼   cup lime juice

    Optional toppings:
    Chopped jalapeños,
    chopped red onion and
    crumbled queso fresco

1. Press saute function; select pork setting. Press timer; set to 15 minutes. Start. Cook and stir chorizo, onion, poblanos and jalapeños in inner pot until chorizo is cooked through. Press cancel. Drain; return chorizo mixture to inner pot.

2. Stir in tomato paste. Add potatoes, tomatoes, beans, stock and spices; stir to combine. Cover with glass lid. Press slow cook; select pork setting. Select short cook time (6 hours). Start. Cook until potatoes are tender.

3. Stir in lime juice. If desired, serve with optional toppings.

1 CUP: *263 cal., 9g fat (3g sat. fat), 25mg chol., 823mg sod., 33g carb. (11g sugars, 6g fiber), 12g pro.*

COCONUT-LIME CHICKEN CURRY SOUP

PREP: 15 MIN. | **SLOW-COOK:** 6¼ HOURS | **MAKES:** 8 SERVINGS (2½ QT.)

2 cans (13.66 oz. each) light coconut milk

2 cans (4 oz. each) chopped green chiles

8 green onions, sliced

2 tsp. grated lime zest

½ cup lime juice

¼ cup sweet chili sauce

6 garlic cloves, minced

4 tsp. curry powder

½ tsp. salt

2 lbs. boneless skinless chicken thighs, cut into ½-in. pieces

3 cups cooked basmati rice

Minced fresh cilantro

1. Place the first 9 ingredients into inner pot; stir in chicken. Cover with glass lid. Press slow cook function; select poultry setting. Set to medium cook time (6 hours). Start. Cook until chicken is tender.

2. Skim fat; stir in cooked rice. Cook, covered, 15-30 minutes longer or until heated through. Sprinkle servings with cilantro.

1¼ CUPS: *356 cal., 16g fat (7g sat. fat), 76mg chol., 455mg sod., 28g carb. (7g sugars, 2g fiber), 23g pro.*

Chicken thighs are great additions to soup because the meat stays juicy and moist, and they have a richer, more robust flavor than boneless skinless chicken breasts.

COMFORTING BEEF STEW

PREP: 20 MIN. | **SLOW-COOK:** 10 HOURS | **MAKES:** 8 SERVINGS (2 QT.)

1½ lbs. beef stew meat, cut into 1-in. cubes

3 Tbsp. all-purpose flour

3 Tbsp. canola oil

1½ lbs. russet potatoes, peeled and cubed

6 medium carrots, cut into 1-in. lengths

1 medium onion, coarsely chopped

3 celery ribs, coarsely chopped

1 can (14½ oz.) diced tomatoes, undrained

½ to 1 cup beef broth

1 tsp. ground mustard

½ tsp. salt

½ tsp. pepper

½ tsp. dried thyme

1. Toss together stew meat and flour. Press saute function; select beef setting. Brown meat in oil in batches. Remove; layer potatoes, carrots, onion and celery in inner pot. Top with beef.

2. In a large bowl, combine tomatoes, broth, mustard, salt, pepper and thyme. Pour over beef. Cover with glass lid. Press slow cook function; select beef setting. Select long cook time (10 hours). Start. Cook until beef and vegetables are tender.

1 CUP: *269 cal., 12g fat (3g sat. fat), 53mg chol., 365mg sod., 23g carb. (6g sugars, 4g fiber), 19g pro.*

"The message I'm trying to get across is, it doesn't have to take three days to do this. With planning, you can do a lot and really have quality food every day."

PORK HOMINY STEW

PREP: 15 MIN. | **SAUTE:** 8 MIN. | **PRESSURE-COOK:** 10 MIN. + RELEASING
MAKES: 8 SERVINGS (2 QT.)

1 Tbsp. canola oil

1 lb. boneless pork shoulder butt roast, cubed

2 medium tomatoes, seeded and chopped

1 can (15 oz.) hominy, rinsed and drained

1 cup minced fresh cilantro

1 medium onion, chopped

4 green onions, chopped

1 jalapeño pepper, seeded and chopped

2 garlic cloves, minced

1 Tbsp. chili powder

1 tsp. ground cumin

½ tsp. cayenne pepper

½ tsp. coarsely ground pepper

6 cups chicken broth

Optional toppings: Corn tortillas, chopped onion, minced fresh cilantro and lime wedges

1. Press saute function; select pork setting. Press timer; set to 8 minutes. Start. Heat oil in inner pot. Add pork. Cook and stir until browned. Remove pork; drain. Return pork to inner pot.

2. Add next 12 ingredients. Lock pressure lid. Press pressure function; select custom. Press timer; set to 10 minutes. Start.

3. Let pressure release naturally for 5 minutes; quick-release any remaining pressure. If desired, serve with tortillas, onion, cilantro and lime wedges.

1 CUP: *163 cal., 8g fat (2g sat. fat), 37mg chol., 1029mg sod., 10g carb. (2g sugars, 3g fiber), 12g pro.*

Jalapeño peppers contribute fiery excitement to dishes. Leaving in the seeds amps up the heat even more. If that's simply not your taste, consider using the milder poblano for flavor without the spice.

LAMB PITAS WITH YOGURT SAUCE

PREP: 25 MIN. | **SAUTE:** 15 MIN. | **SLOW-COOK:** 8 HOURS | **MAKES:** 8 SERVINGS

2	Tbsp. olive oil
2	lbs. lamb stew meat (¾-in. pieces)
1	large onion, chopped
1	garlic clove, minced
⅓	cup tomato paste
½	cup dry red wine
2	tsp. minced fresh oregano
2	tsp. minced fresh basil
1¼	tsp. salt, divided
½	tsp. ground cumin
¼	tsp. ground coriander
1	medium cucumber
1	cup plain yogurt
16	pita pocket halves, warmed
4	plum tomatoes, sliced

1. Press saute function; select pork setting. Press timer; set to 15 minutes. Start. Heat oil; brown lamb in batches. Remove lamb and keep warm. In drippings, saute onion until tender, 4-6 minutes. Add garlic and tomato paste; cook and stir 2 minutes. Stir in wine, oregano, basil, 1 tsp. salt, cumin and coriander. Add lamb; stir to coat. Press cancel.

2. Cover with glass lid. Press slow cook function; select pork setting. Set to medium cook time (8 hours). Start. Cook until lamb is tender.

3. Dice enough cucumber to measure 1 cup; thinly slice remaining cucumber. Combine diced cucumber with yogurt and remaining ¼ tsp. salt. Fill pita halves with lamb mixture, tomatoes, sliced cucumbers and yogurt mixture.

2 FILLED PITA HALVES: *383 cal., 11g fat (3g sat. fat), 78mg chol., 766mg sod., 39g carb. (5g sugars, 3g fiber), 31g pro.*

✳ *When buying lamb, always look for cuts that are pinkish red in color. Avoid packages of lamb stew meat with excessive liquid. It's a sign that the meat is not as fresh as you'd like.*

VEGETARIAN MANCHESTER STEW

PREP: 15 MIN. | **SAUTE:** 15 MIN. | **PRESSURE-COOK:** 3 MIN. + RELEASING
MAKES: 6 SERVINGS

2   Tbsp. olive oil

2   medium onions, chopped

2   garlic cloves, minced

1   tsp. dried oregano

1   cup dry red wine

1   lb. small red potatoes, quartered

1   can (16 oz.) kidney beans, rinsed and drained

½   lb. sliced fresh mushrooms

2   medium leeks (white portion only), sliced

1   medium carrot, sliced

2½ cups water

1   can (14½ oz.) diced tomatoes

1   tsp. dried thyme

½   tsp. salt

¼   tsp. pepper

    Fresh basil leaves

1. Press saute function; select vegetables setting. Press timer; set to 15 minutes. Start. Heat oil in inner pot. Add onions; cook and stir until crisp-tender, 2-3 minutes. Add garlic and oregano; cook and stir 1 minute longer. Stir in wine. Bring to a boil; cook until liquid is reduced by half, 3-4 minutes. Press cancel.

2. Add potatoes, beans, mushrooms, leeks and carrot. Stir in water, tomatoes, thyme, salt and pepper. Lock pressure lid. Press pressure function; select vegetables setting. Press timer; set to 3 minutes. Start.

3. Let pressure release naturally for 10 minutes; quick-release any remaining pressure. Top with basil.

1⅔ CUPS: *227 cal., 5g fat (1g sat. fat), 0 chol., 460mg sod., 39g carb. (9g sugars, 8g fiber), 9g pro.*

ITALIAN SAUSAGE & KALE SOUP

PREP: 10 MIN. | **SAUTE:** 10 MIN. | **PRESSURE-COOK:** 10 MIN. + RELEASING
MAKES: 8 SERVINGS (3½ QT.)

1	lb. bulk hot Italian sausage
6	cups chopped fresh kale
2	cans (15½ oz. each) great northern beans, rinsed and drained
1	can (28 oz.) crushed tomatoes
4	large carrots, finely chopped (about 3 cups)
1	medium onion, chopped
3	garlic cloves, minced
2	tsp. minced fresh oregano
¼	tsp. salt
⅛	tsp. crushed red pepper flakes
⅛	tsp. pepper
5	cups chicken stock
	Grated Parmesan cheese

1. Press saute function; select pork setting. Press timer; set to 10 minutes. Add sausage to inner pot. Cook and stir, crumbling sausage, until meat is no longer pink. Press cancel. Remove sausage; drain. Return sausage to inner pot.

2. Stir in next 11 ingredients. Lock pressure lid. Press pressure function; select custom. Set to short cook time (10 minutes). Start.

3. Let pressure release naturally for 5 minutes; quick-release any remaining pressure. Top each serving with cheese.

1¾ CUPS: *297 cal., 13g fat (4g sat. fat), 31mg chol., 1105mg sod., 31g carb. (7g sugars, 9g fiber), 16g pro.*

How to Trim Kale

1. If your kale is thin and tender, pull the leaves from the stems or remove them with kitchen shears.

2. If the stems are thicker, place on a cutting board, fold the leaf in half and use a knife to slice away the stem. Discard the stem. Carefully chop leaves as desired or as instructed in the recipe at hand.

HERB & CHEESE-STUFFED BURGERS

PREP: 20 MIN. | **AIR-FRY:** 15 MIN | **MAKES:** 4 SERVINGS

2   green onions, thinly sliced

2   Tbsp. minced fresh parsley

4   tsp. Dijon mustard, divided

3   Tbsp. dry bread crumbs

2   Tbsp. ketchup

½   tsp. salt

1   Tbsp. chopped fresh cilantro

2   tsp. chopped fresh chives

1   lb. lean ground beef
    (90% lean)

2   oz. cheddar cheese, sliced

4   hamburger buns, split

    Optional toppings: Lettuce
    leaves, tomato slices and
    mayonnaise

1. In a small bowl, combine green onions, parsley and 2 tsp. mustard. In another bowl, mix bread crumbs, ketchup, salt, cilantro, chives and remaining 2 tsp. mustard. Add beef to bread crumb mixture; mix lightly but thoroughly.

2. Shape mixture into 8 thin patties. Place sliced cheese in center of 4 patties; spoon green onion mixture over cheese. Top with remaining patties, pressing edges together firmly, taking care to seal completely.

3. Place tall wire rack into inner pot. Arrange patties on rack. Cover with air frying lid. Press air fry function; select custom setting. Press timer; set to 8 minutes. Start.

4. Turn burgers over. Air-fry 6-8 minutes longer or until a thermometer reads 160°. Serve burgers on buns. If desired, add tomato slices, lettuce and mayonnaise.

1 BURGER: *394 cal., 16g fat (7g sat. fat), 85mg chol., 919mg sod., 29g carb. (6g sugars, 1g fiber), 30g pro.*

HEARTY HOMEMADE CHICKEN NOODLE SOUP

PREP: 20 MIN. | **SLOW-COOK:** 6½ HOURS | **MAKES:** 12 SERVINGS (3 QT.)

3 medium carrots, sliced

4 celery ribs, cut into
½-in. pieces

¾ cup finely chopped onion

1 Tbsp. minced fresh
parsley

½ tsp. pepper

¼ tsp. cayenne pepper

1½ tsp. mustard seed

2 garlic cloves, peeled
and halved

1¼ lbs. boneless skinless
chicken breast halves

1¼ lbs. boneless skinless
chicken thighs

4 cans (14½ oz. each)
chicken broth

1 pkg. (9 oz.) refrigerated
linguine

Coarsely ground pepper
and additional minced
fresh parsley, optional

1. Combine the first 6 ingredients in inner pot. Place mustard seed and garlic on a double thickness of cheesecloth; bring up corners of cloth; tie with kitchen string to form a bag. Place in inner pot. Add chicken and broth. Cover with glass lid. Press slow cook function; select poultry setting. Set to medium cook time (6 hours). Start.

2. Discard spice bag. Remove chicken to a cutting board. Stir linguine into inner pot. Cover with glass lid. Press slow cook function; select poultry setting. Press timer; set to 30 minutes. Press temp; set to 212°. Start. Cook until noodles are tender.

3. Cut chicken into pieces and return to soup; heat through. If desired, sprinkle with coarsely ground pepper and additional parsley.

1 CUP: *199 cal., 5g fat (1g sat. fat), 72mg chol., 693mg sod., 14g carb. (2g sugars, 1g fiber), 22g pro.*

SPICY PORTUGUESE CACOILA

PREP: 20 MIN. + MARINATING | **SLOW-COOK:** 8 HOURS | **MAKES:** 12 SERVINGS

4 lbs. boneless pork shoulder butt roast, cut into 2-in. pieces

1½ cups dry red wine

4 garlic cloves, minced

4 bay leaves

1 Tbsp. salt

1 Tbsp. paprika

2 to 3 tsp. crushed red pepper flakes

1 tsp. ground cinnamon

1 large onion, chopped

½ cup water

12 bolillos, split, optional

1. Place pork in a large bowl; add wine, garlic and seasonings. Turn to coat; cover and refrigerate overnight.

2. Transfer pork mixture to inner pot; add onion and water. Cover with glass lid. Press slow cooker function; select pork setting. Set to medium cook time (8 hours). Start. Cook until pork is tender; remove to cutting board.

3. Skim fat from cooking juices. Remove bay leaves. Shred meat with 2 forks; return to pot. If desired, serve on bolillos with a slotted spoon.

1 SANDWICH: *490 cal., 20g fat (7g sat. fat), 90mg chol., 1075mg sod., 38g carb. (6g sugars, 2g fiber), 34g pro.*

"Growing up, I was in a Portuguese festival band. Thinking back on those days conjures up my first memories of connecting food with happy people and good music."

SEAFOOD CIOPPINO

PREP: 20 MIN. | **SLOW-COOK:** 4½ HOURS | **MAKES:** 8 SERVINGS (2½ QT.)

1   can (28 oz.) diced tomatoes, undrained

2   medium onions, chopped

3   celery ribs, chopped

1   bottle (8 oz.) clam juice

½   cup white wine

3   Tbsp. tomato paste

5   garlic cloves, minced

1   Tbsp. olive oil

1   to 2 tsp. Italian seasoning

1   bay leaf

½   tsp. sugar

1   lb. haddock fillets, cut into 1-in. pieces

1   lb. uncooked shrimp (41-50 per lb.), peeled and deveined

8   oz. fresh crabmeat

1   can (6 oz.) chopped clams, undrained

2   Tbsp. minced fresh parsley

1. Combine the first 11 ingredients in inner pot. Cover with glass lid. Press slow cook function; select vegetables setting. Press timer; set to 4 hours. Start.

2. Stir in seafood. Cook, covered, 20-30 minutes longer or until fish just begins to flake easily with a fork and shrimp turn pink. Remove bay leaf. Stir in parsley.

1¼ CUPS: *195 cal., 3g fat (1g sat. fat), 138mg chol., 567mg sod., 11g carb. (5g sugars, 3g fiber), 29g pro.*

Chopping an Onion

To quickly chop an onion, peel and cut it in half from the root to the top. Leaving the root attached, place the flat side down on the work surface. Cut vertically through the onion, leaving the root end uncut. Cut across the onion, discarding root end. The closer the cuts, the more finely the onion will be chopped.

CHICKEN & TURKEY

Delicious, easy and straightforward, these enticing entrees will turn any meal into an unforgettable experience.

STUFFED TURKEY WITH MOJO SAUCE

PREP: 30 MIN. | **SLOW-COOK:** 5 HOURS + STANDING | **AIR-FRY:** 10 MIN.
MAKES: 12 SERVINGS (ABOUT 1 CUP SAUCE)

1 medium green pepper, finely chopped

1 medium onion, finely chopped

2 garlic cloves, minced

2 tsp. ground coriander

1 tsp. ground cumin

⅛ tsp. cayenne pepper

1 lb. uncooked chicken sausage links, casings removed

1 fresh boneless turkey breast (4 lbs.)

¼ tsp. salt

¼ tsp. pepper

MOJO SAUCE

1 cup orange juice

½ cup fresh cilantro leaves

¼ cup minced fresh oregano or 4 tsp. dried oregano

¼ cup lime juice

4 garlic cloves, minced

1 tsp. ground cumin

½ tsp. pepper

¼ tsp. salt

⅛ tsp. cayenne pepper

¼ cup olive oil

1. In a bowl, combine first 6 ingredients. Crumble sausage over mixture; mix well. With skin side down, pound turkey breast with a meat mallet to ½-in. thickness. Sprinkle with salt and pepper. Spread sausage mixture over turkey to within 1 in. of edges. Roll up jelly-roll style, starting with a short side; tie at 1½- to 2-in. intervals with kitchen string. Place in inner pot.

2. In a blender, combine first 9 sauce ingredients; cover and process until blended. While processing, gradually add oil in a steady stream. Pour over turkey.

3. Cover with glass lid. Press slow cook function; select poultry setting. Press timer; set to 5 hours. Start. Cook until a thermometer inserted in center of turkey reads 165°.

4. Cover with air frying lid. Press air fry function; select custom setting. Press timer; set to 10 minutes. Start. Remove from inner pot; cover and let stand roughly 10 minutes before slicing. Discard string.

5. Meanwhile, skim fat from cooking juices. Press saute function; select poultry setting. Start. Bring to a boil; cook until liquid is reduced by half. Serve with turkey.

1 SLICE WITH 2 TBSP. SAUCE: *719 cal., 46g fat (9g sat. fat), 174mg chol., 515mg sod., 7g carb. (4g sugars, 1g fiber), 66g pro.*

CHIPOTLE-LIME CHICKEN THIGHS

PREP: 15 MIN. | **SOUS VIDE:** 45 MIN. | **AIR-FRY:** 15 MIN. | **MAKES:** 4 SERVINGS

2 garlic cloves, peeled

¾ tsp. salt

1 Tbsp. lime juice

1 Tbsp. minced chipotle
pepper in adobo sauce

2 tsp. adobo sauce

1 tsp. chili powder

4 bone-in chicken thighs
(about 1½ lbs.)

1. Add water to inner pot. Cover with glass lid. Press sous vide function; select poultry setting. Press timer; set to short cook time (1 hour). Press temperature; set to 140°.

2. Place garlic on a cutting board; sprinkle with salt. Using the flat side of a knife, mash garlic. Continue to mash until it reaches a paste consistency; transfer to a small bowl. Stir in the lime juice, pepper, adobo sauce and chili powder. Gently loosen skin from chicken thighs; rub garlic mixture under skin. Transfer to a sealable bag, removing as much air as possible.

3. When water has reached 110°, add chicken. Cover with glass lid. Cook chicken 1 hour (chicken will appear undercooked).

4. Remove chicken; empty inner pot and wipe dry. Place tall wire rack into inner pot. Remove chicken from bag and arrange in a single layer on rack. Cover with air frying lid. Press air fry function; select poultry setting. Press timer; set to 15 minutes. Start. Cook until a thermometer inserted in thickest part of thigh reads 170°-175°.

1 CHICKEN THIGH: *244 cal., 15g fat (4g sat. fat), 81mg chol., 605mg sod., 2g carb. (1g sugars, 0 fiber), 23g pro.*

Fresh Garlic Made Easy
Using the flat side of a chef's knife, crush a garlic clove. Peel away the skin. Then use flat side of the knife once again to mash the garlic.

CHICKEN WITH OLIVES & ARTICHOKES

PREP: 30 MIN. | **PRESSURE-COOK:** 15 MIN. + RELEASING | **MAKES:** 8 SERVINGS

¼ cup all-purpose flour

½ tsp. garlic salt

¼ tsp. pepper

8 bone-in chicken thighs (3 lbs.), skin removed if desired

1 Tbsp. olive oil

4 garlic cloves, thinly sliced

1 Tbsp. grated lemon zest

1 tsp. dried thyme

½ tsp. dried rosemary, crushed

1 can (14 oz.) water-packed quartered artichoke hearts, drained

½ cup pimiento-stuffed olives

1 bay leaf

1½ cups orange juice

¾ cup chicken broth

2 Tbsp. honey

GREMOLATA

¼ cup minced fresh basil

1 tsp. grated lemon zest

1 garlic clove, minced

1. In a shallow bowl, mix flour, garlic salt and pepper. Dip chicken thighs in flour mixture to coat both sides; shake off excess. Press saute function; select poultry setting. Heat oil in inner pot. Brown chicken in batches on all sides. Return all chicken to inner pot.

2. Sprinkle garlic, lemon zest, thyme and rosemary over chicken. Top with artichoke hearts, olives and bay leaf. In a bowl, mix orange juice, broth and honey; pour over top. Lock pressure lid. Press pressure function; select poultry setting. Press timer; set to 15 minutes. Start.

3. Let pressure release naturally for 10 minutes; quick-release any remaining pressure. Remove bay leaf; transfer chicken and artichoke mixture to a serving platter. Mix gremolata ingredients in a small bowl; sprinkle over chicken.

1 CHICKEN THIGH WITH 2 TBSP. ARTICHOKE MIXTURE AND 1½ TSP. GREMOLATA: *293 cal., 13g fat (3g sat. fat), 87mg chol., 591mg sod., 17g carb. (9g sugars, 0 fiber), 26g pro.*

BACON HERB TURKEY BREAST

PREP: 25 MIN. | **PRESSURE-COOK:** 15 MIN. + RELEASING | **AIR-FRY:** 15 MIN.
MAKES: 6 SERVINGS

3 thick-sliced bacon strips

5 garlic cloves, minced

1 Tbsp. chopped fresh sage

1½ tsp. chopped fresh rosemary

1 tsp. chopped fresh oregano

1 tsp. chopped fresh thyme

3 Tbsp. unsalted
   butter, softened

1 tsp. kosher salt, divided

1 tsp. freshly ground
   pepper, divided

1 bone-in turkey breast
   (3½ to 4 lbs.)

1 cup chicken broth

1 Tbsp. cornstarch

1 Tbsp. cold water

1. Press saute function; select pork setting. Press timer; set to 5 min. Start. Cook bacon until crisp; press cancel. Transfer to paper towels to drain, reserving 1 Tbsp. of rendered bacon fat. Finely chop cooled bacon; transfer to a small bowl. Add garlic, sage, rosemary, oregano, thyme, butter, ½ tsp. salt and ½ tsp. pepper. Mix thoroughly to form a paste.

2. Using your fingertips, gently loosen turkey breast skin. Spread paste under skin. Season outside of turkey breast with remaining ½ tsp. salt and ½ tsp. pepper. Brush turkey all over with reserved bacon fat.

3. Pour broth into inner pot. Place turkey on wire rack with handles; use handles to lower into inner pot. Lock pressure lid. Select pressure function; set to poultry setting. Press timer; set to 15 minutes. Start.

4. Let pressure release naturally for 10 minutes; quick-release any remaining pressure. Cover with air frying lid. Press air fry function; select poultry setting. Press timer; set to 15 minutes. Start. Cook until a thermometer inserted in turkey breast reads at least 170°.

5. Remove turkey from pressure cooker; tent with foil. Let stand 10 minutes before slicing. Meanwhile, skim fat from the cooking juices. Press saute function; select poultry setting. Press timer; set to 10 minutes. Start.

6. Bring the cooking juices to a boil. In a small bowl, mix cornstarch and water until smooth; stir into cooking juices. Return to a boil, stirring constantly; cook and stir until thickened, 1-2 minutes. Serve with turkey.

1 SERVING: *536 cal., 31g fat (12g sat. fat), 172mg chol., 744mg sod., 3g carb. (0 sugars, 0 fiber), 58g pro.*

NASHVILLE HOT CHICKEN

PREP: 30 MIN. | **AIR-FRY:** 10 MIN./BATCH | **MAKES:** 6 SERVINGS

2 **Tbsp. dill pickle juice, divided**

2 **Tbsp. hot pepper sauce, divided**

1 **tsp. salt, divided**

2 **lbs. chicken tenderloins**

1 **cup all-purpose flour**

½ **tsp. pepper**

1 **large egg**

½ **cup buttermilk**

Olive oil spray

½ **cup olive oil**

2 **Tbsp. cayenne pepper**

2 **Tbsp. dark brown sugar**

1 **tsp. paprika**

1 **tsp. chili powder**

½ **tsp. garlic powder**

Dill pickle slices

1. In a bowl or shallow dish, combine 1 Tbsp. pickle juice, 1 Tbsp. hot sauce and ½ tsp. salt. Add chicken and turn to coat. Refrigerate, covered, at least 1 hour. Drain, discarding any marinade.

2. In a shallow bowl, mix flour, ½ tsp. salt and pepper. In another shallow bowl, whisk egg, buttermilk, remaining 1 Tbsp. pickle juice and remaining 1 Tbsp. hot sauce. Dip chicken in flour to coat both sides; shake off excess. Dip in egg mixture, then again in flour mixture.

3. Place tall wire rack in inner pot. Arrange chicken in a single layer on rack; spritz chicken with olive oil spray. Cover with air frying lid. Press air fry function; select custom setting. Press timer; set to 10 minutes. Start. Cook until golden brown, 5-6 minutes.

4. Turn; spritz with additional olive oil spray. Cook until golden brown, 5-6 minutes longer. Whisk together remaining ingredients; pour over hot chicken. Serve with pickles.

5 OZ. COOKED CHICKEN: *413 cal., 21g fat (3g sat. fat), 96mg chol., 170mg sod., 20g carb. (5g sugars, 1g fiber), 39g pro.*

"Let's kick it up a notch!"

PHYLLO CHICKEN POTPIE

PREP: 35 MIN. | **PRESSURE-COOK:** 6 MIN. | **AIR-FRY:** 25 MIN. | **MAKES:** 6 SERVINGS

2 medium red potatoes, cut into 1-in. cubes

2 cups frozen pearl onions

1 cup sliced fresh mushrooms

1 cup reduced-sodium chicken broth

1½ lbs. boneless skinless chicken breasts, 1-in. cubes

½ lb. fresh asparagus, trimmed and cut into 1-in. pieces

3 Tbsp. cornstarch

3 Tbsp. sherry or additional reduced-sodium chicken broth

1½ tsp. minced fresh thyme

½ tsp. salt

¼ tsp. pepper

10 sheets phyllo dough (14x9 in.)

Olive oil spray

1. Add potatoes, onions, mushrooms and chicken broth to inner pot; top with chicken. Lock pressure lid. Press pressure function; select poultry setting. Press timer; set to 6 minutes. Start.

2. Quick-release pressure. Add the asparagus. Press saute function; select poultry setting. Combine cornstarch and sherry until smooth; stir into mixture. Bring to a boil; cook and stir 2 minutes or until thickened. Press cancel. Stir in thyme, salt and pepper. Transfer mixture to a 2-qt. baking dish (dish must fit inside inner pot). Wipe inner pot clean.

3. Place 1 sheet of phyllo dough on a work surface; spritz with olive oil spray. Layer with remaining phyllo sheets, spritzing each layer. (Keep remaining phyllo covered with plastic wrap and a damp towel to prevent it from drying out.) Arrange over chicken mixture, crumpling so it fits on top; spritz again.

4. Cut two 20x3-in. strips of heavy-duty foil; crisscross so they resemble an "X." Place dish in center of "X"; use strips as handles to lower dish into inner pot. Cover with air frying lid. Press air fry function; select bake setting. Set to short cook time (25 minutes). Start. Filling should be bubbly and topping golden brown. Use foil strips as handles to remove baking dish.

1 CUP: *300 cal., 8g fat (1g sat. fat), 63mg chol., 481mg sod., 26g carb. (4g sugars, 2g fiber), 27g pro.*

LEMON CILANTRO CHICKEN

PREP: 25 MIN. | **SLOW-COOK:** 4 HOURS | **AIR-FRY:** 25 MIN. | **MAKES:** 6 SERVINGS

½ cup chopped fresh cilantro

3 Tbsp. canola oil, divided

2 Tbsp. lemon juice

2 garlic cloves, minced

2 tsp. salt

1 tsp. grated lemon zest

1 broiler/fryer chicken (3 to 4 lbs.)

½ tsp. paprika

½ tsp. pepper

½ cup white wine or chicken broth

Flaked sea salt, optional

1. In a small bowl, combine cilantro, 2 Tbsp. oil, lemon juice, garlic, salt and lemon zest. Loosen skin around chicken breast, leg and thigh. Rub cilantro mixture under skin. Rub any remaining mixture into the cavity. Drizzle with remaining 1 Tbsp. oil. Sprinkle with paprika and pepper.

2. Place chicken on wire rack with handles. Lower into inner pot; add wine. Cover with glass lid. Press slow cook function; select poultry setting. Set to short cook time (4 hours). Start.

3. Remove glass lid. Cover with air frying lid. Press air fry function; select poultry setting. Press timer; set to 25 minutes. Start. Chicken should reach 170°-175° and be lightly browned. If desired, sprinkle with flaked sea salt before serving.

1 SERVING: *375 cal., 24g fat (5g sat. fat), 104mg chol., 878mg sod., 2g carb. (0 sugars, 0 fiber), 33g pro.*

Three Ways to Zest a Lemon

1. Use a rasp—a hand-held grater that makes ready-to-use, superfine zest.

2. Using the finest side of a box grater, carefully zest the lemon. Be sure not to grate down to the pale-colored pith.

3. With a citrus zester, make narrow strips of zest and then mince finely with a knife.

SOUTHERN-STYLE CHICKEN

PREP: 15 MIN. | **AIR-FRY:** 15 MIN./BATCH | **MAKES:** 4 SERVINGS

2 cups crushed Ritz®
  crackers (about 50)

1 Tbsp. minced fresh parsley

1 Tbsp. Emeril's®
  Original Essence

½ cup all-purpose flour

2 large eggs, beaten

1 Tbsp. water

4 bone-in chicken thighs

4 chicken drumsticks

  Olive oil spray

1. In a shallow bowl, mix cracker crumbs, parsley and Emeril's Original Essence. Place flour in a separate shallow bowl. Add eggs and water to a third shallow bowl; beat lightly. Dip chicken in flour to coat both sides; shake off excess. Dip in egg mixture, then in crumb mixture, patting to help coating adhere.

2. Place tall wire rack into inner pot. Arrange chicken in a single layer on greased rack. Spritz chicken with olive oil spray. Cover with air frying lid. Press air fry function; select poultry setting. Press timer; set to 10 minutes. Start.

3. Turn chicken over. Spritz with olive oil spray. Air fry 5-10 minutes longer or until chicken is golden brown and juices run clear. Repeat with remaining chicken.

1 CHICKEN THIGH AND 1 DRUMSTICK: *582 cal., 30g fat (8g sat. fat), 221mg chol., 381mg sod., 32g carb. (3g sugars, 1g fiber), 44g pro.*

"If you can understand a culture, then you understand the food. If you can understand the food, you understand the people."

TURKEY IN CREAM SAUCE

PREP: 20 MIN. | **SLOW-COOK:** 8 HOURS | **MAKES:** 8 SERVINGS

1¼ cups white wine

1 medium onion, chopped

2 garlic cloves, minced

2 bay leaves

2 Tbsp. minced fresh rosemary

½ tsp. pepper

3 turkey breast tenderloins (¾ lb. each)

3 Tbsp. cornstarch

½ cup half-and-half

½ tsp. salt

1. Combine wine, onion, garlic and bay leaves in inner pot. Combine rosemary and pepper; rub over turkey. Place in inner pot. Cover with glass lid. Press slow cook function; select poultry setting. Press timer; set to 8 hours. Start. Cook until turkey is tender.

2. Remove turkey to a serving platter; keep warm. Strain and skim fat from cooking juices. Press saute function; select poultry setting. Bring liquid to a boil. Combine cornstarch, half-and-half and salt until smooth. Gradually stir into simmering liquid. Bring to a boil; cook and stir for 2 minutes or until thickened. Serve with turkey.

1 SERVING: *205 cal., 3g fat (1g sat. fat), 58mg chol., 231mg sod., 6g carb. (1g sugars, 0 fiber), 32g pro.*

* *Out of half-and-half? Try combining 4½ tsp. melted butter with enough whole milk to equal 1 cup.*

GREEN CHILE TURKEY SOFT TACOS

PREP: 10 MIN. | **SLOW-COOK:** 6 HOURS | **MAKES:** 4 SERVINGS

2 lbs. turkey thighs
  or drumsticks

1 can (8 oz.) tomato sauce

1 can (4 oz.) chopped
  green chiles

⅓ cup chopped onion

2 Tbsp. Worcestershire sauce

1 to 2 Tbsp. chili powder

2 garlic cloves, minced

¾ tsp. ground cumin

8 flour tortillas (6 in.),
  warmed

Optional toppings:
Chopped green onions,
olives, chopped tomatoes,
shredded cheddar cheese,
sour cream and shredded
lettuce

1. Remove skin from turkey; add to inner pot. In a small bowl, combine tomato sauce, chiles, onion, Worcestershire sauce, chili powder, garlic and cumin; pour over turkey. Cover with glass lid. Press slow cook function; select poultry setting. Set to medium cook time (6 hours). Start. Cook until turkey is tender.

2. Remove turkey; shred meat with a fork and return to inner pot. Heat through.

3. Spoon about ½ cup of turkey mixture down the center of each tortilla. Add toppings of your choice. Fold bottom of tortilla over filling and roll up.

2 TACOS: *536 cal., 21g fat (7g sat. fat), 114mg chol., 1018mg sod., 41g carb. (4g sugars, 5g fiber), 44g pro.*

SMOKY PAPRIKA CHICKEN

PREP: 10 MIN. | **PRESSURE-COOK:** 30 MIN. | **AIR-FRY:** 25 MIN. | **MAKES:** 4 SERVINGS

1 medium onion, chopped

4 bone-in chicken breast halves (3 lbs.)

2 Tbsp. all-purpose flour

1 cup chicken broth

1 Tbsp. tomato paste

1 to 2 garlic cloves, minced

1 Tbsp. smoked paprika

½ tsp. salt

½ tsp. dried thyme

Dash hot pepper sauce

1 cup sour cream

1. Add onion to inner pot; top with chicken. In a small bowl, combine flour and broth until smooth. Whisk in tomato paste, garlic, paprika, salt, thyme and hot pepper sauce. Pour over chicken. Lock pressure lid. Press pressure function; select poultry setting. Set to medium cook time (30 minutes). Start.

2. Quick-release pressure. Remove chicken. Stir sour cream into cooking juices; remove and keep warm. Wipe inner pot clean.

3. Place chicken on wire rack with handles; lower into inner pot. Cover with air frying lid. Press air fry function; select poultry setting. Press timer; set to short cook time (25 minutes). Cook until lightly browned. Serve chicken with reserved sauce.

1 SERVING: *548 cal., 28g fat (11g sat. fat), 181mg chol., 706mg sod., 10g carb. (4g sugars, 1g fiber), 62g pro.*

The difference between regular paprika and smoked paprika is simple yet important. Whereas regular paprika is made of crushed dried chiles, smoked paprika starts with chiles that are smoked, often over an oak fire, and then crushed into a seasoning that's sensational for nearly any poultry dish.

BEEF

You can't beat the hearty goodness of a beef dinner. From classics like ribeyes and meat loaf to exciting flavors from around the globe, these recipes are sure to become new staples in your home.

CUBAN ROPA VIEJA

PREP: 25 MIN. | **PRESSURE-COOK:** 12 MIN. + RELEASING | **MAKES:** 8 SERVINGS

6 bacon strips, chopped

2 beef flank steaks
  (1 lb. each), cut in half

1 can (28 oz.) crushed
  tomatoes

2 cups beef stock

1 can (6 oz.) tomato paste

5 garlic cloves, minced

1 Tbsp. ground cumin

2 tsp. dried thyme

¾ tsp. salt

½ tsp. pepper

1 medium onion,
  thinly sliced

1 medium sweet pepper,
  sliced

1 medium green pepper,
  sliced

¼ cup minced fresh
  cilantro

  Hot cooked rice

1. Press saute function; select beef setting. Cook bacon until crisp, stirring occasionally. Remove with a slotted spoon; drain on paper towels. In drippings, brown steak in batches. Return bacon to inner pot. Press cancel.

2. In a large bowl, combine tomatoes, beef stock, tomato paste, garlic, seasonings, onions and peppers; pour over meat. Lock pressure lid. Press pressure function; select custom setting. Press timer; set to 12 minutes. Start.

3. Let pressure release naturally for 10 minutes; quick-release any remaining pressure. Shred beef with 2 forks; return to inner pot to heat through. Stir in cilantro. Serve over rice with a slotted spoon.

1 SERVING: *331 cal., 17g fat (6g sat. fat), 68mg chol., 753mg sod., 16g carb. (9g sugars, 4g fiber), 29g pro.*

✳ | *Ropa vieja is a mouthwatering favorite in Cuban cuisine. The tender shredded beef is flavored with juicy tomatoes and a variety of herbs and seasonings. Try it alongside a helping of black beans.*

BISCUIT-TOPPED SHORT RIBS

PREP: 45 MIN. | PRESSURE-COOK: 1 HOUR | AIR-FRY: 13 MIN. | MAKES: 8 SERVINGS

½ cup all-purpose flour plus 2 Tbsp., divided

1¼ tsp. salt, divided

½ tsp. pepper

2 lbs. well-trimmed boneless beef short ribs, cut into 1½-in. pieces

5 Tbsp. olive oil, divided

1 large onion, chopped

1 medium carrot, chopped

1 celery rib, chopped

1 garlic clove, minced

2 Tbsp. tomato paste

4 cups beef stock

1 cup dry red wine or additional beef stock

1 tsp. poultry seasoning

1 bay leaf

1 pkg. (14 oz.) frozen pearl onions, thawed

4 medium carrots, cut into 2-in. pieces

BISCUIT TOPPING

2 cups all-purpose flour

4 tsp. baking powder

2 tsp. sugar

½ tsp. salt

½ tsp. cream of tartar

½ cup cold butter, cubed

⅔ cup 2% milk

Fresh thyme leaves

1. In a shallow bowl, mix ½ cup flour, ¾ tsp. salt and pepper. Dip short ribs in flour mixture to coat all sides; shake off excess. Press saute function; select beef setting. Heat 3 Tbsp. oil in inner pot. Brown beef in batches. Remove from insert.

2. Add remaining 2 Tbsp. oil, onion, chopped carrot and celery; cook and stir until tender, 2-3 minutes. Add garlic; cook 1 minute longer. Stir in tomato paste and remaining 2 Tbsp. flour until blended. Gradually stir in stock and wine until smooth. Return beef to inner pot; stir in poultry seasoning, bay leaf and remaining ½ tsp. salt. Bring to a boil.

3. Lock pressure lid. Press pressure function; select custom setting. Set to long cook time (60 minutes). Start.

4. Quick-release pressure. Stir in pearl onions and carrot pieces. Lock pressure lid. Press pressure function; select vegetables setting. Press timer; set to 2 minutes. Start.

5. Quick-release pressure. In a small bowl, mix the first 5 biscuit topping ingredients. Cut in butter until crumbly. Gently stir in milk (mixture will be very thick). Drop by scant ¼ cupfuls over beef mixture. Cover with air frying lid. Press air fry function; select bake setting. Press timer; set to 13 minutes. Start. Cook until a toothpick inserted in biscuits comes out clean. Sprinkle with thyme before serving.

1 SERVING: *543 cal., 30g fat (13g sat. fat), 78mg chol., 975mg sod., 44g carb. (9g sugars, 3g fiber), 23g pro.*

BEEF & BEAN CHIMICHANGAS

PREP: 25 MIN. | **SAUTE:** 10 MIN. | **AIR-FRY:** 8 MIN./BATCH | **MAKES:** 8 CHIMICHANGAS

¾ lb. ground beef

1 small onion, chopped

1 small green pepper, chopped

1 jalapeño pepper, seeded and minced

3 garlic cloves, minced

1 can (16 oz.) refried beans

¼ cup shredded cheddar cheese

¼ cup taco sauce

1 tsp. Emeril's® Southwest Spice Blend

8 flour tortillas (10 in.)

2 Tbsp. melted butter

Optional toppings: Shredded lettuce, sour cream, chopped tomatoes and additional cheddar cheese

1. Press saute function; select beef setting. Cook ground beef, onion, green pepper, jalapeño and garlic until beef is no longer pink, 7-10 minutes, breaking up beef into crumbles; drain. Add the beans, cheese, taco sauce and spice blend. Cook and stir until cheese is melted, about 3 minutes. Press cancel.

2. Spoon about ⅓ cup beef mixture off-center on each tortilla. Fold up edge nearest filling; fold in both sides and roll up. Brush with butter. Wipe inner pot clean.

3. Place tall wire rack in inner pot. Place 2 chimichangas seam side down on rack. Close air frying lid. Press air fry function; select bake setting. Press timer; set to 8 minutes. Start. Repeat with remaining chimichangas. Serve with toppings of your choice.

1 CHIMICHANGA: *401 cal., 16g fat (7g sat. fat), 37mg chol., 914mg sod., 46g carb. (4g sugars, 5g fiber), 17g pro.*

Home Ground

1. Experience the incredible flavor of beef you've ground yourself. Freeze 1 lb. chuck roast for 15 minutes. Cut the frozen meat into small cubes.

2. Place the cubes in a food processor. Pulse 20 to 22 times until the meat is coarsely ground.

CARIBBEAN POT ROAST

PREP: 30 MIN. | **PRESSURE-COOK:** 55 MIN. + RELEASING | **MAKES:** 10 SERVINGS

1   Tbsp. canola oil

1   boneless beef chuck
    roast (2½ lbs.), halved

½   cup water

2   medium sweet
    potatoes, cubed

2   large carrots, sliced

1   large onion, chopped

¼   cup chopped celery

1   can (15 oz.) tomato sauce

2   garlic cloves, minced

1   Tbsp. all-purpose flour

1   Tbsp. sugar

1   Tbsp. brown sugar

1   tsp. ground cumin

¾   tsp. salt

¾   tsp. ground coriander

¾   tsp. chili powder

¾   tsp. grated orange zest

¾   tsp. baking cocoa

½   tsp. dried oregano

⅛   tsp. ground cinnamon

1. Press saute function; select beef setting. Heat 1½ tsp. oil to inner pot. Brown 1 roast half on all sides. Remove; repeat with remaining beef and oil. Remove beef.

2. Add water; cook 30 seconds, stirring to loosen browned bits from pan. Add sweet potatoes, carrots, onion and celery; top with beef. In a large bowl, combine remaining ingredients; pour over top.

3. Lock pressure lid. Press pressure function; select beef setting. Press timer; set to 55 minutes. Start.

4. Let pressure release naturally. A thermometer inserted in beef should read at least 145°.

3 OZ. COOKED BEEF WITH ½ CUP VEGETABLE MIXTURE: *282 cal., 13g fat (4g sat. fat), 74mg chol., 442mg sod., 18g carb. (8g sugars, 3g fiber), 24g pro.*

MEDITERRANEAN RIBEYES

PREP: 15 MIN. | **SOUS VIDE:** 1 HOUR | **AIR-FRY:** 10 MIN. | **MAKES:** 4 SERVINGS

4 garlic cloves, minced

½ tsp. salt

⅛ tsp. pepper

2 beef ribeye steaks
   (12 oz. each and at
   least 1 in. thick)

3 Tbsp. chopped fresh basil

1 Tbsp. minced fresh oregano

2 tsp. olive oil

2 tsp. lemon juice

2 Tbsp. crumbled feta cheese

   Kalamata olives and lemon
   slices, optional

1. Add water to inner pot. Cover with glass lid. Press sous vide function; select poultry setting. Press timer; set to short cook time (1 hour). Press temp; set to 110°.

2. Meanwhile, rub garlic, salt and pepper over steaks. Sprinkle with herbs; pressing to adhere. Place steaks in a sealable bag, removing as much air as possible. When the water has reached 110°, add steaks. Cover with glass lid. Cook 1 hour (steak will appear undercooked).

3. Remove steaks from bag; empty inner pot and wipe dry. Place tall wire rack inside inner pot. Arrange steaks in single layer on rack. Drizzle with olive oil. Cover with air frying lid. Press air fry function; select beef setting. Press timer; set to 10 minutes. Press temp; adjust to 392°. Start. Add additional cooking time as desired for doneness (for medium-rare, a thermometer should read 135°; medium, 140°; medium-well, 145°).

4. Transfer to a serving platter. Drizzle with lemon juice and sprinkle with cheese. If desired, top with olives and garnish with lemon.

½ STEAK: *406 cal., 30g fat (12g sat. fat), 102mg chol., 407mg sod., 2g carb. (0 sugars, 0 fiber), 31g pro.*

"The best way to ensure steak is cooked the way you like it is to test it with a meat thermometer. There's no crime in using a thermometer when you cook. All of the cooks in my kitchen, including me, carry them."

SMOKY GARLIC MEAT LOAF

PREP: 25 MIN. | **SLOW-COOK:** 4 HOURS | **MAKES:** 8 SERVINGS

6 Tbsp. ketchup, divided

2 Tbsp. Worcestershire sauce

12 saltines, crushed

1 medium onion, finely chopped

6 garlic cloves, minced

1 tsp. paprika

½ tsp. salt

½ tsp. pepper

⅛ tsp. cayenne pepper

2 lbs. lean ground beef (90% lean)

1. Cut three 20x3-in. strips of heavy-duty foil; crisscross so they resemble spokes of a wheel. Place strips on the bottom and up the sides of inner pot. Coat strips with cooking spray.

2. In a large bowl, combine 2 Tbsp. ketchup, Worcestershire sauce, saltines, onion, garlic, paprika, salt, pepper and cayenne. Crumble beef over mixture and mix well. Shape into a round loaf. Place in the center of the strips.

3. Cover with glass lid. Press slow cook function; select beef setting. Press timer; set to 5 hours. Start. Cook until a thermometer reads 160°. Using foil strips as handles, remove the meat loaf to a platter. Spread remaining ketchup over top.

1 SLICE: *221 cal., 10g fat (4g sat. fat), 71mg chol., 450mg sod., 9g carb. (4g sugars, 1g fiber), 23g pro.*

Easy Does It

1. When making meat loaf, always crumble the beef over the crumb-seasoning mixture first.

2. Use your hands to gently combine the ingredients. Overworking the mixture can lead to a tough and chewy meat loaf.

SPICY BEEF & PEPPER CORNBREAD BAKE

PREP: 15 MIN. | **SAUTE:** 10 MIN. | **AIR-FRY:** 20 MIN. | **MAKES:** 8 SERVINGS

1½ lbs. ground beef

1 medium onion, chopped

1 large green pepper, chopped

3 cans (8 oz. each) tomato sauce

6 garlic cloves, minced

2 tsp. chili powder

½ tsp. salt

½ tsp. pepper

¼ tsp. cayenne pepper

CORNBREAD

1 cup all-purpose flour

¾ cup cornmeal

3 Tbsp. sugar

1 Tbsp. baking powder

½ tsp. salt

1 large egg, beaten

1 cup whole milk

¼ cup canola oil

Sour cream and minced fresh cilantro, optional

1. Press saute function; select beef setting. Cook beef, onion and green pepper until beef is no longer pink, 7-10 minutes, breaking up beef into crumbles; drain. Add tomato sauce, garlic, chili powder, salt, pepper and cayenne; simmer 5-10 minutes. Press cancel.

2. Meanwhile, in a large bowl, combine flour, cornmeal, sugar, baking powder and salt. In another bowl, combine egg, milk and oil; stir into dry ingredients just until moistened. Pour over beef mixture.

3. Close air frying lid. Press air fry function; select custom setting. Press timer; set to 20 minutes. Start. Cook until a toothpick inserted into cornbread comes out clean. If desired, serve with sour cream and cilantro.

1 SERVING: *410 cal., 20g fat (5g sat. fat), 79mg chol., 957mg sod., 37g carb. (9g sugars, 3g fiber), 21g pro.*

WINE-BRAISED BEEF SHANKS

PREP: 30 MIN. | **PRESSURE-COOK:** 40 MIN. + RELEASING | **MAKES:** 6 SERVINGS

3 beef shanks (14 oz. each)

1 tsp. salt

1 tsp. canola oil

1 small onion, chopped

1 medium carrot, chopped

1 medium green
   pepper, chopped

1 cup dry red wine
   or beef broth

1 cup beef broth

1 lemon slice

1 Tbsp. cornstarch

1 Tbsp. water

1. Sprinkle beef with salt. Press saute function; cook beef in oil in batches until browned. Press cancel. Add onion, carrot, green pepper, wine, broth and lemon to shanks in inner pot.

2. Lock pressure lid. Press pressure function; select beef setting. Press timer; set to 40 minutes. Start.

3. Let pressure release naturally for 10 minutes; quick-release any remaining pressure. Remove meat and vegetables; keep warm. Discard lemon.

4. Skim fat from cooking juices. Press saute function; select beef setting. In a small bowl, mix cornstarch and water until smooth; stir into cooking juices. Simmer, stirring constantly, until thickened, 1-2 minutes. Serve with the beef and vegetables.

3 OZ. COOKED BEEF WITH ½ CUP SAUCE: *172 cal., 5g fat (2g sat. fat), 51mg chol., 592mg sod., 5g carb. (2g sugars, 1g fiber), 23g pro.*

* *Beef shanks come from the upper leg portion of the animal. Generally tougher cuts of meat, they cook to tender perfection when prepared with a moist-heat cooking technique such as pressure cooking.*

PORK

*"Pork fat rules!" was a popular motto on Emeril Live, and it's easy
to see why. From shredded pork and classic chops to ribs slathered in
sauce, you'll turn to these irresistible entrees time and again.*

ANDOUILLE-STUFFED PORK LOIN

PREP: 35 MIN. | **PRESSURE-COOK:** 30 MIN. | **AIR-FRY:** 10 MIN. | **MAKES:** 6 SERVINGS

2 Tbsp. Dijon mustard

1 Tbsp. apricot preserves

1½ tsp. minced fresh
    rosemary or ½ tsp.
    dried rosemary, crushed

1½ tsp. minced fresh thyme
    or ½ tsp. dried thyme

2 garlic cloves, minced

1 boneless pork loin
   roast (2 lbs.)

½ tsp. salt

½ tsp. pepper

2 fully cooked andouille
   sausage links
   (about ½ lb.)

6 bacon strips

¼ cup chicken broth

¼ cup white wine

1. In a small bowl, combine the first 5 ingredients. Set aside.

2. Make a lengthwise slit down the center of roast to within ½ in. of bottom. Open roast so it lies flat; cover with plastic wrap. Flatten slightly. Remove plastic wrap. Season with salt and pepper.

3. Arrange 2 sausage links in center of roast. Close roast; brush with mustard mixture. Wrap roast with bacon. Tie several times with kitchen string. Pour broth and wine into inner pot. Place roast on wire rack with handles; lower into inner pot. Lock pressure lid. Press pressure function; select pork setting. Set to medium cook time (30 minutes). Start.

4. Let pressure release naturally for 10 minutes; quick-release any remaining pressure. Cover with air frying lid. Press air fry function; select custom setting. Press timer; set to 10 minutes. Start. A thermometer inserted into pork should read at least 145° and the bacon should be lightly crisp. Let stand 5 minutes before slicing. Discard string.

5 OZ. COOKED MEAT: *339 cal., 18g fat (6g sat. fat), 133mg chol., 841mg sod., 4g carb. (1g sugars, 0 fiber), 40g pro.*

✳ | *Save yourself a bit of time (and cleanup) by asking
the butcher to flatten or butterfly the pork loin for you.*

BALSAMIC SMOKED PORK CHOPS

PREP: 15 MIN. | **AIR-FRY:** 12 MIN./BATCH | **MAKES:** 4 SERVINGS

2 large eggs

¼ cup 2% milk

1 cup panko bread crumbs

1 cup finely chopped pecans

4 smoked bone-in pork chops (7½ oz. each)

¼ cup all-purpose flour

Olive oil spray

GLAZE

⅓ cup balsamic vinegar

2 Tbsp. brown sugar

2 Tbsp. fig jam

1 Tbsp. frozen orange juice concentrate, thawed

1. In a shallow bowl, whisk together eggs and milk. In another shallow bowl, toss bread crumbs with pecans. Coat pork chops with flour; shake off excess. Dip in egg mixture, then in crumb mixture, patting to help adhere.

2. Place tall wire rack into inner pot. Arrange pork chops in a single layer on rack. Spritz with olive oil spray. Cover with air frying lid. Press air fry function; select custom setting. Press timer; set to 6 minutes. Start.

3. Turn chops. Spritz with olive oil spray. Air-fry 6-9 minutes longer or until golden brown. Repeat with remaining pork chops. Meanwhile, place glaze ingredients in a small saucepan; bring to a boil. Cook and stir until slightly thickened, 6-8 minutes; strain sauce if desired. Serve with chops.

1 PORK CHOP WITH 1 TBSP. GLAZE: *579 cal., 36g fat (10g sat. fat), 106mg chol., 1374mg sod., 36g carb. (22g sugars, 3g fiber), 32g pro.*

CAJUN SPICED PORK LOIN

PREP: 10 MIN. | **PRESSURE-COOK:** 30 MIN. | **AIR-FRY:** 10 MIN. | **MAKES:** 16 SERVINGS

4 tsp. Emeril's® Cajun
   Seasoning Blend, divided

1 boneless pork loin
   roast (3½ to 4 lbs.)

4 cups cubed peeled
   sweet potatoes

1 medium onion, chopped

½ cup chicken broth

3 garlic cloves, minced

1. Rub 3 tsp. Cajun seasoning over roast. Add the remaining ingredients to inner pot; top with roast. Lock pressure lid. Press pressure function; select pork setting. Set to medium cook time (30 minutes). Start.

2. Let pressure release naturally for 10 minutes; quick-release any remaining pressure. Remove roast; transfer vegetable mixture to a bowl; mash until smooth. Set aside; keep warm. Wipe inner pot clean.

3. Place roast on wire rack with handles. Use handles to lower into inner pot. Cover with air frying lid. Press air fry function; select custom setting. Press timer; set to 10 minutes. Start. Cook until a meat thermometer reads 145°. Let stand for 5-10 minutes before slicing. Serve with sweet potato mixture.

3 OZ. COOKED PORK WITH ½ CUP VEGETABLE MIXTURE: *156 cal., 5g fat (2g sat. fat), 50mg chol., 211mg sod., 8g carb. (2g sugars, 1g fiber), 20g pro.*

CARNITAS

PREP: 15 MIN. | **PRESSURE-COOK:** 30 MIN. + RELEASING | **AIR-FRY:** 10 MIN.
MAKES: 16 SERVINGS

1	boneless pork shoulder roast (4 lbs.), cut into 2-in. cubes
1	tsp. salt
1	tsp. pepper
6	large garlic cloves, minced
½	cup fresh cilantro leaves, chopped
3	large navel oranges
1	large lemon
¼	cup bacon drippings or canola oil
16	flour tortillas (8 in.), warmed
	Optional toppings: Chopped tomatoes, shredded cheddar cheese, sliced green onions, sour cream and sliced avocado

1. Place pork in inner pot. Season with salt and pepper; sprinkle with garlic and cilantro. Squeeze juice from the oranges and lemon over meat. Lock pressure lid. Press pressure function; select pork setting. Set to medium cook time (30 minutes). Start.

2. Let pressure release naturally for 10 minutes; quick-release any remaining pressure. With a slotted spoon, remove meat; drain well on paper towels. Discard cooking liquid; wipe inner pot clean.

3. Toss meat with bacon drippings. Add to mesh basket; place into inner pot. Cover with air frying lid. Press air fry function; select custom setting. Press timer; set to 10 minutes. Start. Cook until lightly browned and edges are crispy.

4. Serve warm in tortillas with toppings of your choice.

1 SERVING: *377 cal., 17g fat (6g sat. fat), 69mg chol., 455mg sod., 32g carb. (3g sugars, 3g fiber), 24g pro.*

To quickly yet gently remove cilantro leaves, run a fork along the stems. (This also works for parsley.) Now you're ready to chop the leaves for your dish.

CHAR SIU PORK

PREP: 25 MIN. + MARINATING | **PRESSURE-COOK:** 1¼ HOURS + RELEASING
MAKES: 8 SERVINGS

½ cup honey

½ cup hoisin sauce

¼ cup soy sauce

¼ cup ketchup

4 garlic cloves, minced

4 tsp. minced fresh gingerroot

1 tsp. Chinese five-spice powder

1 boneless pork shoulder butt roast (3 to 4 lbs.)

½ cup chicken broth

Fresh cilantro leaves

1. Combine the first 7 ingredients; pour into a large bowl. Cut roast in half; add to bowl and turn to coat. Cover; refrigerate overnight.

2. Transfer pork and marinade to inner pot. Add chicken broth. Lock pressure lid. Press pressure function; select pork setting. Press timer; set to 75 minutes. Start.

3. Let pressure release naturally for 10 minutes, then quick-release any remaining pressure.

4. Remove pork; when cool enough to handle, shred meat using 2 forks. Skim fat from cooking juices. Return pork to inner pot. Press saute function; select pork setting. Press timer; set to 5 minutes. Press temp; set to 200°. Start. Cook and stir until heated through. Press cancel. Top pork with the fresh cilantro.

1 SERVING: *392 cal., 18g fat (6g sat. fat), 102mg chol., 981mg sod., 27g carb. (24g sugars, 1g fiber), 31g pro.*

Easy Shredding

It's simple to shred pork shoulder. Use 2 forks to pull the meat in opposite directions. Continue to pull the meat apart until you achieve the desired consistency.

EMERIL'S BABY BACK RIBS

PREP: 10 MIN. | **PRESSURE-COOK:** 30 MIN. + RELEASING | **AIR-FRY:** 10 MIN./BATCH
MAKES: 4 SERVINGS

½ cup water

1½ tsp. cider vinegar

1½ tsp. soy sauce

2½ lbs. pork baby back ribs, cut into serving-size portions

1 Tbsp. Emeril's® Rib Rub

½ cup barbecue sauce, divided

1. Combine water, vinegar and soy sauce in inner pot. Rub ribs with seasoning; add to inner pot. Lock pressure lid. Press pressure function; select ribs setting. Set to medium cook time (30 minutes). Start.

2. Let pressure release naturally for 10 minutes; quick-release any remaining pressure. Remove ribs to a tray; brush with ¼ cup barbecue sauce. Discard cooking liquid. Wipe inner pot clean.

3. Place tall wire rack into inner pot. Arrange ribs in a single layer on rack. Cover with air frying lid. Press air fry function; select custom setting. Press timer; set to 10 minutes. Start. Cook in batches until lightly glazed. Brush with remaining ¼ cup sauce.

1 SERVING: *414 cal., 26g fat (9g sat. fat), 102mg chol., 788mg sod., 14g carb. (11g sugars, 0 fiber), 28g pro.*

"I'm an oven-to-grill guy when it comes to cooking juicy ribs. But this new method also guarantees melt-in-your-mouth tenderness and flavor that will blow you away."

RED BEANS & RICE

PREP: 15 MIN. | **PRESSURE-COOK:** 30 MIN. + RELEASING | **SAUTE:** 10 MIN.
MAKES: 10 SERVINGS

8 cups water

1 pkg. (16 oz.) dried kidney beans (about 2½ cups)

2 cups cubed fully cooked ham (about 1 lb.)

2 bay leaves

2 garlic cloves, minced

1 medium green pepper, chopped

1 medium onion, chopped

2 celery ribs, chopped

12 oz. fully cooked andouille sausage links, sliced

1 tsp. salt

½ to 1 tsp. cayenne pepper

¼ tsp. crushed red pepper flakes

   Hot cooked rice

1. Combine the first 8 ingredients in inner pot. Lock pressure lid. Press pressure function; select beans setting. Set to long cook time (30 minutes). Start. Cook until beans are almost tender.

2. Let pressure release naturally. Stir in sausage, salt, cayenne pepper and red pepper flakes. Press saute function; select vegetables setting. Set to medium cook time (10 minutes). Simmer, stirring constantly, until beans are tender, 7-9 minutes. Remove bay leaves. Serve with rice.

1 CUP BEAN MIXTURE: *197 cal., 2g fat (0 sat. fat), 17mg chol., 587mg sod., 30g carb. (2g sugars, 7g fiber), 17g pro.*

✳ *A mainstay in Cajun dishes, andouille pork sausage is often used in jambalaya and gumbo as well as red beans and rice. Look for it with the packaged meats. If your store is out, kielbasa makes a delicious substitute.*

SWEET SPICED PORK CHOPS

PREP: 15 MIN. | **SOUS VIDE:** 1 HOUR | **AIR-FRY:** 10 MIN. | **MAKES:** 4 SERVINGS

1¼ tsp. mustard seed

1¼ tsp. smoked paprika

1¼ tsp. whole peppercorns

1 tsp. onion powder

1 tsp. garlic powder

½ tsp. kosher salt

¼ tsp. cayenne pepper

1½ tsp. brown sugar

4 bone-in pork loin chops (7 oz. each)

1. Add water to inner pot. Cover with glass lid. Press sous vide function; select pork setting. Press timer; set to short cook time (1 hour). Press temp; set to 125°.

2. Using a mortar and pestle or spice grinder, crush seasonings with brown sugar. Rub mixture over chops, pressing to adhere. Transfer to a sealable bag, removing as much air as possible. When water has reached 125°, add pork. Cover with glass lid. Cook 1 hour (pork will appear undercooked).

3. Remove pork chops from bag. Empty inner pot; wipe dry. Place tall wire rack into inner pot. Arrange chops in a single layer on rack. Cover with air frying lid. Press air fry function; select custom setting. Set to short cook time (10 minutes). Start. A thermometer inserted in pork should read 145°. Let stand 5 minutes before serving.

1 PORK CHOP: *222 cal., 9g fat (3g sat. fat), 86mg chol., 305mg sod., 4g carb. (2g sugars, 1g fiber), 31g pro.*

SEAFOOD & VEGETARIAN

Today's home cooks are turning to fish and seafood for quick and healthy dishes that deliver on taste. Meatless Mondays are making regular appearances in modern meal plans, too. Let these options take your dinnertime lineups to delicious new heights.

SAMBAL SHRIMP

PREP: 20 MIN. | **SOUS VIDE:** 40 MIN. | **MAKES:** 6 SERVINGS

1 cup sambal oelek (ground fresh chili paste)

¼ cup sugar

¼ cup freshly squeezed lime juice

¼ cup olive oil

2 Tbsp. minced garlic

1 tsp. minced fresh gingerroot

2 Tbsp. mirin (sweet rice wine)

1 Tbsp. Vietnamese fish sauce (nuoc nam)

1 Tbsp. dark Asian sesame oil

1½ lbs. uncooked shrimp (16-20 per lb.), peeled and deveined

1 Tbsp. coarsely chopped fresh cilantro

1 Tbsp. coarsely chopped fresh mint

Hot cooked rice or noodles, optional

1. Add water to inner pot. Cover with glass lid. Press sous vide function; select fish setting. Set to medium cook time (40 minutes).

2. In a large bowl, whisk together first 9 ingredients; add sauce mixture and shrimp to sealable bag, removing as much air as possible. When the water has reached 140°, add shrimp. Cover with glass lid. Cook 40 minutes or until shrimp are just firm.

3. Remove shrimp from bag to a serving dish. Sprinkle with cilantro and mint. If desired, serve with rice or noodles.

1 SERVING: *382 cal., 21g fat (2g sat. fat), 151mg chol., 709mg sod., 23g carb. (15g sugars, 0 fiber), 24g pro.*

Peeling & Deveining Shrimp

1. Pull legs and first section of shell to one side. Continue pulling the shell up around the top and to the side. Pull off shell by tail if desired.

2. Remove black vein running down the back of the shrimp by making a shallow slit with a paring knife along the back. Rinse the shrimp under cold water to remove the vein.

CLAM SAUCE

PREP: 10 MIN. | **SAUTE:** 5 MIN. | **PRESSURE-COOK:** 2 MIN. | **MAKES:** 4 CUPS

4 Tbsp. butter

2 Tbsp. olive oil

½ cup finely chopped onion

8 oz. fresh mushrooms, chopped

4 garlic cloves, minced

2 cans (10 oz. each) whole baby clams

½ cup white wine

¼ cup water

2 tsp. lemon juice

1 bay leaf

¾ tsp. dried oregano

½ tsp. crushed red pepper flakes

¼ tsp. salt

¼ tsp. Italian seasoning

2 Tbsp. chopped fresh parsley

Hot cooked pasta

Grated Parmesan cheese, optional

1. Press saute function; select vegetables setting. Press timer; set to 5 minutes. Start. Heat butter and oil in inner pot. Add onion; cook and stir 2 minutes. Add mushrooms and garlic; cook 1 minute longer. Press cancel.

2. Drain the clams, reserving liquid; coarsely chop. Add the clams, the reserved clam juice and the next 8 ingredients to inner pot. Lock pressure lid. Press pressure function; select fish setting. Set to short cook time (2 minutes). Start.

3. Quick-release pressure. Discard bay leaf; stir in parsley. Serve with pasta. If desired, serve with grated Parmesan cheese and additional lemon juice and parsley.

½ CUP: 138 cal., 10g fat (4g sat. fat), 40mg chol., 580mg sod., 5g carb. (1g sugars, 0 fiber), 7g pro.

TOMATO-POACHED HALIBUT

PREP: 15 MIN. | **SAUTE:** 10 MIN. | **PRESSURE-COOK:** 3 MIN. | **MAKES:** 4 SERVINGS

1   Tbsp. olive oil

2   poblano peppers, finely chopped

1   small onion, finely chopped

1   can (14½ oz.) fire-roasted diced tomatoes, undrained

1   can (14½ oz.) diced tomatoes, undrained

½   cup water

¼   cup chopped pitted green olives

3   garlic cloves, minced

¼   tsp. pepper

⅛   tsp. salt

4   halibut fillets (4 oz. each)

⅓   cup chopped fresh cilantro

4   lemon wedges

     Crusty whole grain bread, optional

1. Press saute function; select vegetables setting. Press timer; set to 10 minutes. Start. Heat oil in inner pot. Add poblano peppers and onion; cook and stir until crisp-tender, 2-3 minutes.

2. Stir in tomatoes, water, olives, garlic, pepper and salt; simmer until liquid is reduced by half, 3-4 minutes. Press cancel. Top with fillets. Lock pressure lid. Press pressure function; select fish setting. Set to medium cook time (3 minutes). Start.

3. Quick-release pressure. A thermometer inserted in fish should read at least 145°. Sprinkle with chopped cilantro. Serve with lemon wedges and, if desired, bread.

1 FILLET WITH 1 CUP SAUCE: *215 cal., 7g fat (1g sat. fat), 56mg chol., 614mg sod., 16g carb. (7g sugars, 3g fiber), 23g pro.*

The subtle halibut lets the exciting tastes of poblano peppers, fire-roasted tomatoes and fresh cilantro shine in this easy entree. Serve it alongside a hearty helping of polenta or angel hair pasta.

CHICKPEA & POTATO CURRY

PREP: 25 MIN. | **SAUTE:** 15 MIN. | **PRESSURE-COOK:** 3 MIN. + RELEASING
MAKES: 6 SERVINGS

1   Tbsp. canola oil

1   medium onion, chopped

2   garlic cloves, minced

2   tsp. minced fresh
    gingerroot

2   tsp. ground coriander

1   tsp. garam masala

1   tsp. chili powder

½   tsp. salt

½   tsp. ground cumin

¼   tsp. ground turmeric

2½ cups vegetable stock

2   cans (15 oz. each)
    chickpeas or garbanzo
    beans, rinsed and drained

1   can (15 oz.) crushed
    tomatoes

1   large baking potato,
    peeled and cut into
    ¾-in. cubes

1   Tbsp. lime juice

    Chopped fresh cilantro

    Hot cooked rice

    Sliced red onion and lime
    wedges, optional

1. Press saute function; select vegetables setting. Press timer; set to 15 minutes. Start. Heat oil in inner pot. Add onion; cook and stir until crisp-tender, about 3 minutes. Add garlic, ginger and dry seasonings; cook and stir 1 minute.

2. Add stock to inner pot. Cook 30 seconds, stirring to loosen browned bits from pan. Press cancel. Stir in chickpeas, tomatoes and potato. Lock pressure lid. Press pressure function; select custom setting. Press timer; set to 3 minutes. Start.

3. Let pressure release naturally for 10 minutes; quick-release any remaining pressure.

4. Stir in lime juice; sprinkle with cilantro. Serve with rice and, if desired, red onion and lime wedges.

1¼ CUPS: *240 cal., 6g fat (0 sat. fat), 0 chol., 767mg sod., 42g carb. (8g sugars, 9g fiber), 8g pro.*

＊   *When you're finished making this recipe, save the extra ginger. Unpeeled gingerroot can be frozen in a resealable plastic freezer bag for up to 1 year. When needed, simply peel and grate the ginger, or chop the required amount.*

CRISPY FISH & FRIES

PREP: 15 MIN. | **AIR-FRY:** 32 MIN. | **MAKES:** 4 SERVINGS

1 lb. potatoes
 (about 2 medium)

2 Tbsp. olive oil

¼ tsp. salt

¼ tsp. pepper

FISH

⅓ cup all-purpose flour

¼ tsp. pepper

1 large egg

2 Tbsp. water

⅔ cup crushed cornflakes

1 Tbsp. grated
 Parmesan cheese

⅛ tsp. cayenne pepper

1 lb. haddock or cod fillets

¼ tsp. salt

 Tartar sauce, optional

1. Peel and cut potatoes lengthwise into ½-in.-thick slices; cut slices into ½-in.-thick sticks. In a large bowl, toss potatoes with oil, salt and pepper.

2. Arrange potatoes in a single layer in mesh basket; place into inner pot. Cover with air frying lid. Press air fry function; select custom setting. Press timer; set to 7 minutes. Start.

3. Stir fries. Air-fry 5-10 minutes longer or until fries are lightly browned and crisp. Repeat with remaining potatoes.

4. Meanwhile, in a shallow bowl, mix flour and pepper. In another shallow bowl, whisk egg with water. In a third bowl, toss cornflakes with cheese and cayenne. Sprinkle fish with salt; dip into flour mixture to coat both sides; shake off excess. Dip in egg mixture, then in cornflake mixture, patting to help coating adhere.

5. Remove fries and basket; cover to keep warm. Place tall wire rack into inner pot. Arrange fish in a single layer on rack. Cover with air frying lid. Press air fry function; select custom setting. Press timer; set to 4 minutes. Start.

6. Turn fish. Air-fry 4-6 minutes longer or until fish is lightly browned and just beginning to flake easily with a fork. Do not overcook. Return fries to basket to heat through. Serve immediately. If desired, serve with tartar sauce.

1 SERVING: *312 cal., 9g fat (2g sat. fat), 85mg chol., 503mg sod., 35g carb. (3g sugars, 1g fiber), 23g pro.*

SHRIMP & ASPARAGUS RISOTTO

PREP: 20 MIN. | **SAUTE:** 10 MIN. | **PRESSURE-COOK:** 8 MIN. | **MAKES:** 8 SERVINGS

4   Tbsp. unsalted butter, divided

1   small onion, finely diced

9   garlic cloves, minced, divided

1⅔ cups uncooked arborio rice

1   cup white wine

4   cups chicken broth

½   cup shredded Parmesan cheese, divided

3   Tbsp. white wine vinegar

¾   tsp. sugar

½   tsp. Dijon mustard

⅛   tsp. salt

Dash fresh ground pepper

⅓   cup extra virgin olive oil

2   Tbsp. olive oil

2   lbs. uncooked shrimp (26-30 per lb.), peeled and deveined

1   lb. fresh asparagus, trimmed

Salt and pepper to taste

1. Press saute function; select vegetables setting. Press timer; set to 10 minutes. Start. Heat 3 Tbsp. butter in inner pot. Add onion; cook and stir until crisp-tender, 4-5 minutes. Add 6 minced garlic cloves; cook 1 minute longer. Add rice; cook and stir 2 minutes. Stir in ½ cup wine; cook and stir until absorbed. Add remaining ½ cup wine, broth and ¼ cup Parmesan cheese. Press cancel.

2. Lock pressure lid. Press pressure function; select risotto setting. Set to medium cook time (8 minutes). Start. Quick-release pressure. Rice should be tender; stir until mixture is creamy. Transfer to a serving bowl; keep warm. Clean inner pot.

3. In a nonreactive mixing bowl, whisk together vinegar, sugar, mustard, salt and pepper. While whisking, add extra virgin olive oil in a thin, steady stream until completely incorporated and dressing is emulsified; set aside.

4. Press saute function; select vegetables setting. Add olive oil and remaining garlic in inner pot; cook 1 minute. Add shrimp; cook and stir until shrimp begin to turn pink, about 5 minutes. Add remaining 1 Tbsp. butter and olive oil mixture; stir until butter melts. Reduce heat. Add asparagus; cook until tender, 3-5 minutes. Serve over risotto. Season with salt and pepper. Sprinkle with remaining cheese.

1 SERVING: *424 cal., 15g fat (6g sat. fat), 157mg chol., 661mg sod., 39g carb. (3g sugars, 1g fiber), 26g pro.*

"Asparagus makes any dish feel indulgent. A simple yet luxurious pairing of asparagus and shrimp in a creamy risotto makes for a dazzling dinner."

CHEESY BLACK BEAN STUFFED PEPPERS

PREP: 15 MIN. | **PRESSURE-COOK:** 6 MIN. + RELEASING | **MAKES:** 4 SERVINGS

4 medium sweet
   red peppers

1 can (15 oz.) black beans,
   rinsed and drained

1 cup shredded pepper
   jack cheese

¾ cup salsa

1 small onion, chopped

½ cup frozen corn

⅓ cup uncooked
   converted long
   grain rice

1¼ tsp. chili powder

½ tsp. ground cumin

   Sour cream, optional

1. Place wire rack with handles into inner pot. Cut and discard tops from peppers; remove seeds. In a large bowl, mix beans, cheese, salsa, onion, corn, rice, chili powder and cumin; spoon into peppers. Set peppers on rack.

2. Lock pressure lid. Press pressure function; select vegetables setting. Set timer to medium cook time (6 minutes). Start. Cook until tender.

3. Let pressure release naturally. If desired, serve with sour cream.

1 STUFFED PEPPER: *333 cal., 10g fat (5g sat. fat), 30mg chol., 582mg sod., 45g carb. (8g sugars, 8g fiber), 15g pro.*

Converted rice is a home cook's dream come true. Also known as parboiled rice, it has gone through a steam-pressure process before milling. This gives it a firmer grain, helps keep the kernels separate, retains nutrients and makes a hearty filling in recipes like this one.

CREOLE-STYLE STEWED SHRIMP & ANDOUILLE

PREP: 20 MIN. | **SLOW-COOK:** 6¼ HOURS | **MAKES:** 8 SERVINGS

1   can (28 oz.) diced
     tomatoes, undrained

1   lb. fully cooked andouille
     sausage links, cubed

½   lb. boneless skinless
     chicken breasts,
     cut into 1-in. cubes

1   can (8 oz.) tomato sauce

1   cup diced onion

1   small sweet red
     pepper, diced

1   small green pepper, diced

1   cup chicken broth

1   celery rib with
     leaves, chopped

2   Tbsp. tomato paste

2   tsp. dried oregano

2   tsp. Cajun seasoning

1   garlic cloves, minced

2   bay leaves

1   tsp. Louisiana-style
     hot sauce

½   tsp. dried thyme

1   lb. uncooked medium
     shrimp, peeled and deveined

     Hot cooked rice

1. Combine the first 16 ingredients in inner pot. Cover with glass lid. Press slow cook function; select poultry setting. Set to medium cook time (6 hours). Start.

2. Cook until chicken is no longer pink. Stir in shrimp. Cover; cook 30 minutes longer or until shrimp turns pink. Discard bay leaves. Serve with rice.

1 CUP: *281 cal., 13g fat (4g sat. fat), 176mg chol., 1137mg sod., 13g carb. (6g sugars, 3g fiber), 31g pro.*

SAUTE PRESSURE COOKER

STEAMED MUSSELS WITH PEPPERS

PREP: 30 MIN. | **SAUTE:** 8 MIN. | **PRESSURE-COOK:** 2 MIN. | **MAKES:** 4 SERVINGS

2 lbs. fresh mussels, scrubbed and beards removed

2 Tbsp. olive oil

1 jalapeño pepper, seeded and chopped

3 garlic cloves, minced

1 bottle (8 oz.) clam juice

½ cup white wine

⅓ cup chopped sweet red pepper

3 green onions, sliced

1 tsp. minced fresh oregano or ½ tsp. dried oregano

1 bay leaf

2 Tbsp. minced fresh parsley

¼ tsp. salt

¼ tsp. pepper

French bread baguette, sliced, optional

1. Tap mussels; discard any that do not close. Set aside. Press saute function; select vegetables setting. Press timer; set to 8 minutes. Start. Heat olive oil in inner pot. Add jalapeño; cook and stir until crisp-tender, 2-3 minutes. Add garlic; cook 1 minute longer. Press cancel.

2. Stir in mussels, clam juice, wine, red pepper, green onions, oregano and bay leaf. Lock pressure lid. Press pressure function; select fish setting. Set to short cook time (2 minutes). Start.

3. Quick-release pressure. Discard bay leaf and any unopened mussels. Sprinkle with parsley, salt and pepper. If desired, serve with baguette slices.

12 MUSSELS: *293 cal., 12g fat (2g sat. fat), 65mg chol., 931mg sod., 12g carb. (1g sugars, 1g fiber), 28g pro.*

Always clean the sand and grit off mussels before cooking by scrubbing them on both sides with a stiff brush under running cold water. Remove the beard (a tuft of fibers that protrudes from the shell) before cooking. Simply pull the beard toward the shell hinge to remove it. Do not debeard mussels more than 1 hour before cooking.

MUST-TRY SIDES

Your Pressure Air Fryer makes it a snap to prepare side dishes that simmer to perfection on their own so you can focus on the rest of your meal. Rounding out menus has never been easier.

SMOKY WHITE BEANS & HAM

PREP: 15 MIN. | **PRESSURE-COOK:** 30 MIN. + RELEASING | **MAKES:** 10 SERVINGS

1 lb. dried great
  northern beans

3 smoked ham hocks
  (about 1½ lbs.)

3 cans (14½ oz. each)
  chicken broth

2 cups water

2 medium onions,
  chopped

4 garlic cloves, minced

1 to 2 tsp. pepper

¼ to ½ tsp. cayenne
  pepper

  Thinly sliced green
  onions, optional

1. Rinse and sort beans; transfer to inner pot. Add ham hocks. Stir in broth, water, onions, garlic, pepper and cayenne. Lock pressure lid. Press pressure function; select beans setting. Set to long cook time (30 minutes). Start.

2. Let pressure release naturally for 10 minutes; quick-release any remaining pressure. When cool enough to handle, remove meat from bones; cut ham into small pieces and return to inner pot. Serve with a slotted spoon. If desired, sprinkle with green onions.

⅔ CUP: *193 cal., 2g fat (0 sat. fat), 11mg chol., 772mg sod., 31g carb. (3g sugars, 10g fiber), 14g pro.*

"Honestly, I can make a meal just out of sides. And it seems right that home for me now is in the South, where side dishes like this are king."

CHEESY BACON SPAGHETTI SQUASH

PREP: 10 MIN. | **PRESSURE-COOK:** 12 MIN. | **SAUTE:** 15 MIN. | **AIR-FRY:** 7 MIN.
MAKES: 4 SERVINGS

1 **large spaghetti squash (3½ lbs.)**

4 **bacon strips, chopped**

3 **Tbsp. butter**

1 **Tbsp. brown sugar**

½ **tsp. salt**

¼ **tsp. pepper**

¾ **cup shredded Swiss cheese, divided**

1. Halve squash lengthwise; remove and discard seeds. Place wire rack with handles and 1 cup water into inner pot. Place squash on rack. Lock pressure lid. Press pressure function; select vegetables setting. Set to long cook time (12 minutes). Start.

2. Quick-release pressure. Remove squash, rack and water from inner pot; wipe dry. Separate squash into strands with a fork.

3. Press saute function; select pork setting. Press timer; set to 15 minutes. Add bacon; cook and stir until almost crisp. With a slotted spoon, remove the bacon to paper towels. Stir butter, brown sugar, salt and pepper into drippings. Add squash. Cook and stir until heated through. Press cancel. Stir in ½ cup cheese.

4. Transfer squash mixture to a 1½-qt. baking dish; top with bacon and remaining cheese. Clean inner pot. Place dish on wire rack with handles; lower into inner pot. Cover with air frying lid. Press air fry function; select custom. Press timer; set to 7 minutes. Start. Cook until the cheese is melted.

1 CUP: *409 cal., 28g fat (13g sat. fat), 60mg chol., 655mg sod., 32g carb. (4g sugars, 6g fiber), 12g pro.*

CHEDDAR-BROCCOLI CASSEROLE

PREP: 20 MIN. | **STEAM:** 7 MIN. | **SAUTE:** 10 MIN. | **AIR-FRY:** 4 MIN. | **MAKES:** 6 SERVINGS

1   cup chicken broth or water

1   bunch broccoli, cut into
     florets (about 4½ cups)

4½ tsp. cornstarch

¼   tsp. garlic powder

¼   tsp. salt

¼   tsp. pepper

1¾ cups half-and-half

4   oz. cream cheese,
     softened

1   Tbsp. butter

1   cup shredded
     cheddar cheese

TOPPING

½   cup crushed Ritz®
     crackers

2   Tbsp. shredded
     Parmesan cheese

2   Tbsp. butter, melted

1. Place wire rack with handles and chicken broth into inner pot. Add broccoli to mesh basket; place on rack. Cover with glass lid. Press steam function; select vegetables setting. Press timer; set to 7 minutes. Start.

2. Drain and set broccoli aside. In a small bowl, whisk cornstarch, garlic powder, salt and pepper. Gradually whisk in half-and-half until smooth; add to inner pot. Press saute function; select vegetables setting. Set to medium cook time (10 minutes). Bring to a gentle boil, stirring constantly. Cook and stir for 1 minute or until thickened. Stir in cream cheese and butter until melted. Stir in cooked broccoli. Press cancel.

3. Transfer to a 1½-qt. round baking dish. Sprinkle with cheddar cheese. In a small bowl, mix topping ingredients; sprinkle over cheese. Place baking dish on wire rack with handles; lower into inner pot. Cover with air frying lid. Press air fryer function; select custom setting. Press timer; set to 4 minutes. Start. Cook until topping is lightly browned.

¾ CUP: *378 cal., 28g fat (16g sat. fat), 90mg chol., 649mg sod., 18g carb. (6g sugars, 3g fiber), 12g pro.*

CANNED GREEN BEANS

PREP: 10 MIN. | **CANNING:** 20 MIN. | **MAKES:** 4 PINT JARS

2 lbs. fresh green beans, trimmed

2 tsp. canning salt

1. Tightly pack green beans into pint canning jars, leaving 1-in. headspace. Add ½ tsp. canning salt to each jar. Add boiling water to each jar, leaving 1-in. headspace. Remove air bubbles. Wipe rims. Center lids on jars; screw on bands until a little more than fingertip tight.

2. Place wire rack with handles into inner pot. Arrange the jars on rack. Pour hot water into inner pot until water level reaches a quarter of the way up sides of jars. Lock pressure lid. Press canning function. Press timer; set to 20 minutes. Start.

3. Quick-release pressure; remove pressure lid. Let stand 5 minutes before removing from unit to cool further.

4. Lids should be tightly sealed to jars. When jars are completely cool, press center of lid. There should be no give or springing motion. If lid springs or gives, the canning process was not successful. Food must be reprocessed immediately or refrigerated and used within 5 days.

1 CUP: *35 cal., 0 fat (0 sat. fat), 0 chol., 597mg sod., 8g carb. (3g sugars, 4g fiber), 2g pro.*

If the screw bands are too loose, liquid may escape from jars during processing and the seals may fail. If the screw bands are too tight, air cannot vent during processing and food will discolor during storage. Overtightening also may cause lids to buckle and jars to break. Do not use at altitudes exceeding 2,000 feet above sea level.

CHEDDAR GRUYERE MAC & CHEESE

PREP: 15 MIN. | **PRESSURE-COOK:** 3 MIN. | **AIR-FRY:** 7 MIN. | **MAKES:** 12 SERVINGS

16 oz. uncooked elbow macaroni

4 cups water

2 tsp. canola oil

2½ tsp. ground mustard

1 tsp. onion powder

½ tsp. white pepper

¼ tsp. ground nutmeg

2¾ cups half-and-half

½ cup unsalted butter, cubed and divided

1¼ lbs. cheddar cheese, shredded (5 cups)

¾ lb. Gruyere or Emmenthaler cheese, shredded (3 cups)

1 cup crushed Ritz® crackers (about 25 crackers)

Chopped fresh chives

1. Add macaroni, water and oil to inner pot; stir. Lock pressure lid. Press pressure function; select custom. Press timer; set to 3 minutes. Start.

2. Let pressure release naturally for 2 minutes; quick-release any remaining pressure. Whisk ground mustard, onion powder, white pepper and nutmeg into half-and-half. Pour over macaroni. Stir in 4 Tbsp. butter and cheeses until thoroughly combined and melted. Melt remaining 4 Tbsp. butter; stir in cracker crumbs. Sprinkle over macaroni.

3. Cover with air frying lid. Press air fry function; set to custom. Press timer; set to 7 minutes. Start. Cook until crumbs are golden brown. Just before serving, sprinkle with chives.

1 CUP: *635 cal., 42g fat (23g sat. fat), 126mg chol., 603mg sod., 36g carb. (4g sugars, 2g fiber), 27g pro.*

Rich, smooth Gruyere cheese gives dishes a fantastic boost of nutty flavor. If you don't have it on hand, replace it with Emmenthaler cheese or any type of Swiss.

CRISPY FRENCH FRIES

PREP: 15 MIN. | **AIR-FRY:** 12 MIN./BATCH | **MAKES:** 4 SERVINGS

1 lb. potatoes
(about 2 medium)

2 Tbsp. olive oil

¼ tsp. pepper

¼ tsp. salt

1. Peel and cut potatoes lengthwise into ½-in.-thick slices; cut slices into ½-in.-thick sticks. In a large bowl, toss potatoes with oil, pepper and salt.

2. Arrange potatoes in a single layer in mesh basket; place into inner pot. Cover with air frying lid. Press air fry function; select custom. Press timer; set to 7 minutes. Start.

3. Stir fries. Air-fry 5-10 minutes longer or until fries are lightly browned and crisp. Repeat with remaining potatoes. Serve immediately.

1 SERVING: *126 cal., 7g fat (1g sat. fat), 0 chol., 150mg sod., 15g carb. (1g sugars, 1g fiber), 1g pro.*

Handy Kitchen Tip

Use an apple slicer for fast fries. Cut one end off the potato for stability. Stand the potato upright, place the apple slicer on top and gently push down. Presto! Instant fries. Next, use a knife to carefully cut the fries into smaller pieces if the recipe suggests.

SICILIAN STEAMED LEEKS

PREP: 10 MIN. | **PRESSURE-COOK:** 2 MIN. | **MAKES:** 6 SERVINGS

1   **large tomato, chopped**

1   **small navel orange, peeled, sectioned and chopped**

2   **Tbsp. minced fresh parsley**

2   **Tbsp. sliced Greek olives**

1   **tsp. capers, drained**

1   **tsp. red wine vinegar**

1   **tsp. olive oil**

½   **tsp. grated orange zest**

½   **tsp. pepper**

6   **medium leeks (white portion only), halved lengthwise, cleaned**

    Crumbled feta cheese

1. In a bowl, combine the first 9 ingredients; set aside. Place wire rack with handles and 1 cup water into inner pot. Arrange leeks on rack. Lock pressure lid. Press pressure function; select vegetables setting. Set to short cook time (2 minutes). Start.

2. Quick-release pressure. Transfer leeks to a serving platter. Spoon tomato mixture over top; sprinkle with cheese.

1 SERVING: *83 cal., 2g fat (0 sat. fat), 0 chol., 77mg sod., 16g carb. (6g sugars, 3g fiber), 2g pro.*

Cleaning Leeks

1. Remove and discard any withered outer leaves. Give leeks a quick rinse under cold water. Cut off and discard the dark green upper leaves.

2. Cut the leek open lengthwise down one side and rinse again to remove any sandy soil caught between the layers.

3. Chop the leeks into smaller pieces and soak in a bowl of cold water for 30 minutes, stirring occasionally to help remove any additional sand. Drain and use leeks as directed.

RATATOUILLE

PREP: 20 MIN. + STANDING | **SLOW-COOK:** 3 HOURS | **MAKES:** 10 SERVINGS

1 large eggplant, peeled and cut into 1-in. cubes

2 tsp. salt, divided

3 medium tomatoes, chopped

3 medium zucchini, halved lengthwise and sliced

2 medium onions, chopped

1 large green pepper, chopped

1 large sweet yellow pepper, chopped

½ cup kalamata olives or 1 can (6 oz.) pitted ripe olives, drained and chopped

1 can (6 oz.) tomato paste

½ cup minced fresh basil

2 garlic cloves, minced

½ tsp. pepper

2 Tbsp. olive oil

1. Place eggplant in a colander over a plate; sprinkle with 1 tsp. salt and toss. Let stand for 30 minutes. Rinse and drain well. Transfer to inner pot coated with olive oil. Stir in the tomatoes, zucchini, onions, green and yellow peppers, olives, tomato paste, basil, garlic, pepper and remaining salt. Drizzle with olive oil.

2. Cover with glass lid. Press slow cook function; select vegetables setting. Press timer; set to 3 hours. Press temp; set to 212°. Start. Cook until the vegetables are tender.

¾ CUP: *112 cal., 5g fat (1g sat. fat), 0 chol., 464mg sod., 16g carb. (7g sugars, 5g fiber), 4g pro.*

EGGPLANT FRIES

PREP: 15 MIN. | **AIR-FRY:** 10 MIN./BATCH | **MAKES:** 6 SERVINGS

2 **large eggs**

½ **cup grated Parmesan cheese**

½ **cup whole wheat panko bread crumbs**

1 **tsp. Emeril's® Italian Essence**

¾ **tsp. garlic salt**

1 **medium eggplant (about 1¼ lbs.)**

   Olive oil spray

1 **cup meatless pasta sauce, warmed**

1. In a shallow bowl, whisk eggs. In another shallow bowl, mix cheese, panko and seasonings. Trim ends of eggplant; cut eggplant lengthwise into ½-in.-thick slices. Cut slices lengthwise into ½-in. strips. Dip eggplant in eggs, then coat with cheese mixture. Spritz eggplant with olive oil spray.

2. Place tall wire rack into inner pot. Arrange eggplant in a single layer on rack. Cover with air frying lid. Press air fry function; select custom. Press timer; set to 6 minutes. Start.

3. Turn eggplant; spritz with additional olive oil spray. Air-fry 4 minutes longer or until golden brown. Repeat with remaining eggplant. Serve immediately with pasta sauce for dipping.

1 SERVING: *131 cal., 5g fat (2g sat. fat), 68mg chol., 590mg sod., 17g carb. (6g sugars, 4g fiber), 6g pro.*

✳ *Choose eggplants that are firm, heavy and round or pear-shaped. The glossy taut skin should have a uniformly smooth color. When you get it home, store the unwashed eggplant in an open bag in the refrigerator's crisper drawer for up to 3 days.*

GARLIC-ROSEMARY BRUSSELS SPROUTS

PREP: 15 MIN. | **AIR-FRY:** 15 MIN. | **MAKES:** 4 SERVINGS

3 Tbsp. olive oil

2 garlic cloves, minced

½ tsp. salt

¼ tsp. pepper

1 lb. Brussels sprouts, trimmed and halved

½ cup panko bread crumbs

1½ tsp. minced fresh rosemary

1. Place the first 4 ingredients in a small microwave-safe bowl; microwave on high 30 seconds. Toss Brussels sprouts with 2 Tbsp. oil mixture. Add all Brussels sprouts to mesh basket and place into inner pot. Cover with air frying lid. Press air fry function; select custom setting. Press timer; set to 5 minutes. Start.

2. Stir sprouts. Air-fry 7-8 minutes longer or until sprouts are lightly browned and near desired tenderness, stirring halfway through cooking time.

3. Toss bread crumbs with rosemary and remaining oil mixture; sprinkle over sprouts. Air fry 3-5 minutes longer cooking or until crumbs are browned and sprouts are tender. Serve immediately.

¾ CUP: *164 cal., 11g fat (1g sat. fat), 0 chol., 342mg sod., 15g carb. (3g sugars, 4g fiber), 5g pro.*

✳ | *When preparing Brussels sprouts, be sure to remove any loose or yellowed outer leaves. Trim off the stem end and gently rinse the sprouts before beginning the recipe.*

BREAKFAST
& BRUNCH

Breakfast should be a vibrant start to your day, and your Pressure Air Fryer makes things easy. So be bold and experiment with flavors. Sweet. Savory. Spicy. Any one of these simple yet hearty dishes will provide the early energy you need to kick your day up a notch.

BROCCOLI SWISS EGG CUPS

PREP: 15 MIN. | **PRESSURE-COOK:** 6 MIN. | **MAKES:** 4 SERVINGS

7   large eggs

1½ cups half-and-half

3   Tbsp. shredded
    Swiss cheese

2   tsp. minced fresh parsley

1   tsp. minced fresh basil

¼   tsp. salt

⅛   tsp. cayenne pepper

1   to 1½ cups frozen broccoli
    florets, thawed and
    coarsely chopped

1. Whisk 3 eggs with next 6 ingredients; pour into 4 greased 8-oz. canning jars. Divide broccoli among jars; top each with 1 egg. Center lids on jars; screw on bands until fingertip tight.

2. Place wire rack with handles and 1 cup water in inner pot. Place jars on rack. Lock pressure lid. Press pressure function; select egg setting. Set to long cook time (6 minutes). Start.

3. Quick-release pressure. Remove jars. Let stand 3 minutes before serving.

1 SERVING: *274 cal., 19g fat (10g sat. fat), 375mg chol., 333mg sod., 5g carb. (4g sugars, 1g fiber), 16g pro.*

"Talk to me about breakfast and I'll talk to you about eggs. They are the savory blank canvas you can take in most any direction you like."

BANANAS FOSTER GREEK YOGURT

PREP: 20 MIN. + STANDING | **COOK:** 10 HOURS + CHILLING | **MAKES:** ABOUT 1½ QT.

2   qt. pasteurized whole milk

2   Tbsp. plain yogurt with
    live active cultures

BANANAS FOSTER SAUCE

2   Tbsp. unsalted butter

⅓   cup packed brown sugar

¼   tsp. ground cinnamon

    Pinch ground nutmeg

2   medium ripe bananas,
    peeled and sliced

1   Tbsp. banana liqueur

2   Tbsp. dark rum

1   to 2 Tbsp. water

    Sliced ripe bananas and
    toasted walnuts, optional

1. Add milk to inner pot. Cover with glass lid. Press yogurt function; set time to 10 hours. Start. Once the unit reaches 180°, it will stop heating; display will show "cool." Remove glass lid. Once the milk reaches 110°, it will beep; display will show "add."

2. Remove 1 cup milk from inner pot to a small bowl; add yogurt to bowl. Stir until smooth and return all to inner pot. Stir gently to combine. Cover with glass lid.

3. Press yogurt function; start. Incubate, undisturbed, 4-10 hours. The longer it incubates, the thicker and more tangy yogurt will be. A beep will sound when cycle is finished. Transfer inner pot, covered, to refrigerator; do not stir. Chill until cold. If desired, for thicker consistency, strain yogurt through a double layer of cheesecloth or a coffee filter after chilling for 1-2 hours, or until yogurt yields 4 cups.

4. Clean and replace inner pot. Press saute function; select vegetables setting. Add butter; when melted, stir in brown sugar, cinnamon and nutmeg. Cook and stir until sugar dissolves, about 1 minute. Add bananas and banana liqueur. Cook and stir until bananas start to soften and brown, about 2 minutes. Stir in rum. Bring to a boil and cook 1 minute, adding 1-2 Tbsp. of water as necessary to prevent sauce from crystallizing. Remove and cool; stir into yogurt. If desired, serve with fresh sliced bananas and toasted walnuts.

½ CUP: *167 cal., 7g fat (4g sat. fat), 22mg chol., 73mg sod., 18g carb. (16g sugars, 1g fiber), 5g pro.*

CRAB QUICHE BITES

PREP: 15 MIN. | **SOUS VIDE:** 1 HOUR | **MAKES:** 2 SERVINGS

4   large eggs, lightly beaten

3   fresh asparagus spears, cut into ½-in. pieces

½   cup lump crabmeat

¼   cup shredded Swiss cheese

¼   cup 4% cottage cheese

2   Tbsp. chopped green onion

1   tsp. Dijon mustard

½   tsp. Emeril's® Cajun Seasoning Blend

    Dash ground nutmeg

    Olive oil

1. Add water to inner pot. Cover with glass lid. Press sous vide function; select poultry setting. Press timer; set to short cook time (1 hour). Press temp; set to 170°. Start.

2. In a bowl, combine all ingredients except olive oil. Transfer to four 4-oz. canning jars brushed with olive oil. When the water has reached 170°, add jars. (The tops of the jars should be covered by at least 1 in. of water.) Cover with glass lid. Cook for 1 hour or until set. Remove from water and let stand 5 minutes before serving.

1 QUICHE: *255 cal., 14g fat (6g sat. fat), 418mg chol., 535mg sod., 3g carb. (2g sugars, 1g fiber), 26g pro.*

3 Ways to Crack an Egg

1. Gently but firmly, tap the egg squarely against the countertop, creating a crack in the shell. Use your thumbs to press into the crack and separate the shell.

2. Hold an egg in each hand, and tap the eggs together. One egg will crack. Use your thumbs to press into the crack and separate the shell.

3. Using one hand, sharply crack the egg against the side of a bowl. Immediately pull the eggshell apart using your thumb and middle finger.

CARAMELIZED STEEL-CUT OATMEAL WITH BERRIES

PREP: 15 MIN. | **PRESSURE-COOK:** 10 MIN. + RELEASING | **AIR-FRY:** 15 MIN.
MAKES: 3 SERVINGS

3¼ cups water, divided

¾ cup steel-cut oats

¾ cup sweetened shredded coconut

6 Tbsp. dried cranberries

⅜ tsp. each ground cinnamon, cardamom, allspice and nutmeg

⅜ tsp. salt

1½ tsp. butter

3 Tbsp. sugar

3 Tbsp. fresh blueberries

3 Tbsp. fresh raspberries

3 Tbsp. unsweetened coconut flakes

1. Place ¾ cup water, ¼ cup oats, ¼ cup coconut, 2 Tbsp. cranberries and ⅛ tsp. each of cinnamon, cardamom, allspice, nutmeg and salt in each of three 1-pint wide-mouth canning jars. Top each with ½ tsp. butter. Center lids on jars; screw on bands until fingertip tight.

2. Place wire rack with handles and remaining 1 cup water in inner pot. Set jars on rack. Lock pressure lid. Press pressure function; select custom. Set to short cook time (10 minutes). Start.

3. Let pressure release naturally. Remove jars; drain water from inner pot and wipe dry. Unscrew lids from jars, and sprinkle oatmeal with sugar. Place jars in inner pot on wire rack with handles. Cover with air frying lid. Press air fry function; select bake. Press timer; set to 15 minutes. Start. Cook until sugar has caramelized. Serve with berries and toasted coconut.

1 SERVING: *432 cal., 16g fat (11g sat. fat), 5mg chol., 374mg sod., 71g carb. (40g sugars, 8g fiber), 6g pro.*

Prepared in three separate canning jars, this oatmeal is ideal for on-the-go breakfasts. Double up on the recipe during the weekend and store prepared jars in the refrigerator for the week ahead.

PEACH HALVES IN HONEY SYRUP

PREP: 30 MIN. | **CANNING:** 10 MIN./BATCH | **MAKES:** 6 PINT JARS

2 cups water

⅓ cup sugar

¼ cup honey

5 lbs. medium peaches, peeled, pitted and halved

1. Combine water, sugar and honey in the inner pot. Press saute function; select vegetables setting. Bring mixture to a boil. Add peaches; return just to a boil. Press cancel; pack hot peach halves, cut side down, into six 1-pint canning jars, leaving 1-in. headspace. Ladle hot syrup over peaches, leaving 1-in. headspace. Remove air bubbles. Wipe rims. Center lids on jars; screw on bands until a little more than fingertip tight.

2. Clean inner pot; place wire rack with handles in bottom of inner pot. Place filled jars on wire rack, up to 4 jars at a time. Pour hot water into the inner pot with jars until water level reaches one-quarter of the way up sides of jars. Lock pressure lid. Press the canning function. Press timer; set to 10 minutes. Start.

3. Let pressure release naturally for 10 minutes; quick-release any remaining pressure. Carefully remove hot jars; allow to cool to room temperature. Repeat with remaining jars.

4. Lids should be tightly sealed to jars. When jars are completely cool, press center of lid. There should be no give or springing motion. If lid springs or gives, the canning process was not successful. Food must be reprocessed immediately or refrigerated and used within 5 days.

½ CUP: *43 cal., 0 fat (0 sat. fat), 0 chol., 0 sod., 11g carb. (11g sugars, 0 fiber), 0 pro.*

If the screw bands are too loose, liquid may escape from the jars during processing and the seals may fail. If the screw bands are too tight, air cannot vent during processing. Overtightening also may cause lids to buckle and jars to break. Do not use at elevations exceeding 2,000 feet above sea level.

HOMEMADE YOGURT

PREP: 5 MIN. + STANDING | **COOK:** 10 HOURS + CHILLING | **MAKES:** ABOUT 2 QT.

2 qt. pasteurized whole milk

2 Tbsp. plain yogurt with
   live active cultures

1. Add milk to inner pot. Cover with glass lid. Press yogurt function; set time to 10 hours. Start. Once the unit reaches 180°, it will stop heating and the display will show "cool." Remove glass lid. Once the milk reaches 110°, it will beep and the display will show "add."

2. Remove 1 cup milk from inner pot to a small bowl; add yogurt to bowl. Stir until smooth and return all to inner pot. Stir gently to combine. Cover with glass lid.

3. Press yogurt function; start. Incubate, undisturbed, 4-10 hours. The longer it incubates, the thicker and more tangy the yogurt will be. A beep will sound when cycle is finished. Transfer inner pot, covered, to refrigerator; do not stir. Chill until cold.

½ CUP: *76 cal., 4g fat (2g sat. fat), 12mg chol., 53mg sod., 6g carb. (6g sugars, 0 fiber), 4g pro.*

This recipe makes about 8 cups of yogurt, so it's perfect for a parfait bar. Serve the yogurt alongside bowls of granola, berries and cut fruit, and let brunch guests layer their own treat. Don't forget to offer crunchy almonds or sunflower or pumpkin seeds as well as a selection of fruit preserves guests might want to stir into their yogurt parfaits.

CAROLINA SHRIMP & CHEDDAR GRITS

PREP: 15 MIN. | **PRESSURE-COOK:** 10 MIN. + RELEASING | **SAUTE:** 5 MIN.
MAKES: 6 SERVINGS

3 cups water

1 cup half-and-half

1 large garlic clove, minced

½ tsp. salt

¼ tsp. pepper

1 cup uncooked
old-fashioned grits

2 cups shredded
cheddar cheese

¼ cup butter, cubed

1 lb. peeled and deveined
cooked shrimp (31-40 per lb.)

2 medium tomatoes, seeded
and finely chopped

4 green onions, finely chopped

2 Tbsp. minced fresh parsley

4 tsp. lemon juice

2 to 3 tsp. Emeril's®
Cajun Seasoning

1. Combine the first 6 ingredients in inner pot. Lock pressure lid. Press pressure function; select custom. Press timer; set to 10 minutes. Start.

2. Let pressure release naturally for 10 minutes; quick-release any remaining pressure. Stir in cheese and butter until melted. Press saute function; select vegetables setting. Set to medium cook time (10 minutes). Stir in remaining ingredients. Cook 5-10 minutes or until cheese is melted and mixture is heated through. If desired, top with additional parsley.

1 SERVING: *471 cal., 26g fat (15g sat. fat), 193mg chol., 774mg sod., 29g carb. (3g sugars, 2g fiber), 28g pro.*

If you grew up in the South, there's no doubt you're familiar with grits; but if you haven't tried this eye-opening staple yet, what are you waiting for? Made from coarsely ground white corn, grits lend creamy comfort to morning menus, particularly when paired with full-flavored ingredients like shrimp, green onions and cheddar cheese.

CHEESY BREAKFAST EGG ROLLS

PREP: 30 MIN. | **AIR-FRY:** 10 MIN./BATCH | **MAKES:** 12 SERVINGS

½ lb. bulk pork sausage

½ cup shredded sharp cheddar cheese

½ cup shredded Monterey Jack cheese

1 Tbsp. chopped green onion

4 large eggs

1 Tbsp. 2% milk

¼ tsp. salt

⅛ tsp. pepper

1 Tbsp. butter

12 egg roll wrappers

Olive oil spray

Maple syrup or salsa, optional

1. Press saute function; select pork setting. Add sausage to inner pot. Cook sausage until no longer pink, 4-6 minutes, breaking into crumbles; remove to a medium bowl and drain inner pot. Stir cheeses and green onion into sausage; set aside. Wipe inner pot clean.

2. In a small bowl, whisk eggs, milk, salt and pepper until blended. Press saute function; select vegetables setting. Press timer; set to 8 minutes. Melt butter in inner pot. Pour in egg mixture; cook and stir until eggs are thickened and no liquid egg remains. Press cancel. Stir eggs into sausage mixture. Clean inner pot.

3. With corner of an egg roll wrapper facing you, place ¼ cup egg filling just below center of wrapper. (Cover remaining wrappers with a damp paper towel until ready to use.) Fold bottom corner over filling; moisten remaining wrapper edges with water. Fold side corners toward center over filling. Roll up tightly, pressing at tip to seal. Repeat.

4. Place tall wire rack in inner pot. Arrange egg rolls in single layer on rack. Spritz with olive oil spray. Cover with air frying lid. Press air fry function; select custom. Press timer; set to 3 minutes. Start.

5. Turn egg rolls; spritz with olive oil spray. Air-fry 3-4 minutes longer or until golden brown. If desired, serve with maple syrup or salsa.

1 EGG ROLL: *209 cal., 10g fat (4g sat. fat), 87mg chol., 438mg sod., 19g carb. (0 sugars, 1g fiber), 10g pro.*

SHAKSHUKA

PREP: 10 MIN. | **PRESSURE-COOK:** 4 MIN. | **SAUTE:** 20 MIN. | **MAKES:** 4 SERVINGS

2 cans (14½ oz. each)
fire-roasted diced
tomatoes, undrained

1 medium onion, chopped

½ cup water

2 Tbsp. canola oil

2 garlic cloves, minced

2 tsp. smoked paprika

½ tsp. sugar

½ tsp. crushed red
pepper flakes

¼ cup tomato paste

4 large eggs

¼ cup shredded Manchego
or Monterey Jack cheese

2 Tbsp. minced fresh parsley

1 tube (18 oz.) polenta, sliced
and warmed, optional

1. Combine first 8 ingredients in inner pot. Lock pressure lid. Press pressure function; select egg setting. Set to medium cook time (4 minutes). Start.

2. Quick-release pressure. Press saute function; select beef setting. Press timer; set to 25 minutes. Stir in tomato paste; simmer, uncovered, until mixture is slightly thickened, about 10 minutes, stirring occasionally.

3. With the back of a spoon, make 4 wells in sauce. Break an egg into each well; sprinkle with cheese. Cover with glass lid. Simmer until egg whites are completely set and yolks begin to thicken but are not hard, 8-10 minutes. Press cancel. Sprinkle with parsley. If desired, serve with polenta.

1 SERVING: *255 cal., 14g fat (4g sat. fat), 193mg chol., 676mg sod., 20g carb. (9g sugars, 3g fiber), 11g pro.*

Shakshuka originated in the Mediterranean and Middle East. The meal-in-one breakfast features eggs that are poached in a spicy sauce of tomatoes, garlic and onion. Serve it with polenta, toast or simply enjoy it on its own.

LEMON & CORIANDER GREEK YOGURT

PREP: 5 MIN. + STANDING | **COOK:** 10 HOURS + CHILLING | **MAKES:** ABOUT 3 CUPS

2 qt. pasteurized whole milk

2 tsp. grated lemon zest

1 tsp. ground coriander

2 Tbsp. plain yogurt with live active cultures

Honey, optional

1. Add milk, lemon zest and coriander to inner pot. Cover with glass lid. Press yogurt function; set time to 10 hours. Start. Once the unit reaches 180°, it will stop heating and the display will show "cool." Remove glass lid. Once the milk reaches 110°, it will beep and the display will show "add."

2. Remove 1 cup milk from inner pot to a small bowl; add yogurt to bowl. Stir until smooth and return all to inner pot. Stir gently to combine. Cover with glass lid.

3. Press yogurt function; start. Incubate, undisturbed, for 4-10 hours. The longer it incubates, the thicker and more tangy the yogurt will be. A beep will sound when cycle is finished. Transfer inner pot, covered, to refrigerator; do not stir. Chill until cold. Carefully strain the yogurt through a double layer of cheesecloth or a coffee filter after chilling for 4-6 hours or until yogurt yields 3 cups. Serve with honey if desired.

½ CUP: *203 cal., 11g fat (6g sat. fat), 33mg chol., 142mg sod., 16g carb. (16g sugars, 0 fiber), 10g pro.*

SUN-DRIED TOMATO FRITTATA

PREP: 20 MIN. | **PRESSURE-COOK:** 35 MIN. + RELEASING | **MAKES:** 6 SERVINGS

1 Tbsp. olive oil

1 medium Yukon Gold potato, peeled and chopped

1 small onion, thinly sliced

½ cup chopped soft sun-dried tomatoes (not packed in oil)

½ tsp. smoked paprika

12 large eggs

1 tsp. minced fresh thyme or ¼ tsp. dried thyme

1 tsp. hot pepper sauce

½ tsp. salt

¼ tsp. pepper

1 log (4 oz.) fresh goat cheese, coarsely crumbled, divided

1. Press saute function; select vegetables setting. Set to medium cook time (10 minutes). Heat oil in inner pot. Add potato and onion; cook, stirring occasionally, until potato is lightly browned, 5-7 minutes. Stir in tomatoes and paprika. Press cancel. Transfer to a greased round 2-qt. baking dish. Wipe inner pot clean; add 1 cup water to inner pot.

2. In a large bowl, whisk eggs, thyme, hot pepper sauce, salt and pepper; stir in 2 oz. goat cheese. Pour over potato mixture. Top with remaining goat cheese. Cover tightly with foil. Place dish on wire rack with handles; use rack to lower dish into inner pot over water. Lock pressure lid. Press pressure function; select custom setting. Press timer; set to 35 minutes. Start.

3. Let pressure release naturally for 10 minutes; quick-release any remaining pressure.

1 SERVING: *255 cal., 15g fat (6g sat. fat), 389mg chol., 363mg sod., 12g carb. (4g sugars, 2g fiber), 16g pro.*

DESSERTS

From novice bakers to sweet-shop pros, there's a knockout dessert for everyone in this collection. See how a handful of ingredients can surprise, impress and delight everyone at your table.

BREAD PUDDING WITH BOURBON SAUCE

PREP: 15 MIN. | **SLOW-COOK:** 3 HOURS | **MAKES:** 6 SERVINGS

3 large eggs

1¼ cups 2% milk

½ cup sugar

3 tsp. vanilla extract

½ tsp. ground cinnamon

¼ tsp. ground nutmeg

⅛ tsp. salt

4½ cups day-old cubed brioche or egg bread

1¼ cups raisins

BOURBON SAUCE

¼ cup butter, cubed

½ cup sugar

¼ cup light corn syrup

3 Tbsp. bourbon

1. In a large bowl, whisk together first 7 ingredients; stir in bread and raisins. Transfer to inner pot. Cover with glass lid. Press slow cook function; select vegetables setting. Press timer; set to 3 hours. Start.

2. For sauce, place butter, sugar and corn syrup in a small saucepan; bring to a boil, stirring occasionally. Cook and stir until sugar is dissolved. Remove from heat; stir in bourbon. Serve warm with bread pudding.

1 CUP WITH 2 TBSP. SAUCE: *484 cal., 12g fat (7g sat. fat), 117mg chol., 311mg sod., 85g carb. (67g sugars, 2g fiber), 8g pro.*

"Bread pudding has long been a staple in south Louisiana. One reason is because the cooks there are frugal and never waste anything; the other is that it's delicious!"

DUMPLING-TOPPED AMARETTO CHERRIES

PREP: 15 MIN. | **SLOW-COOK:** 4 HRS. | **AIR-FRY:** 10 MIN. | **MAKES:** 10 SERVINGS

4 cans (14½ oz. each) pitted tart cherries

1½ cups sugar

½ cup cornstarch

¼ tsp. salt

½ cup amaretto

DUMPLINGS

1½ cups all-purpose flour

6 Tbsp. sugar

1½ tsp. baking powder

1 tsp. grated lemon zest

¼ tsp. salt

½ cup 2% milk

5 Tbsp. butter, melted

Vanilla ice cream, optional

1. Drain cherries, reserving ½ cup juice. Place cherries in inner pot. In a small bowl, mix sugar, cornstarch and salt; stir in reserved ½ cup juice until smooth. Stir into cherries. Cover with glass lid. Press slow cook function; select vegetables setting. Press timer; set to 3 hours. Start.

2. Stir amaretto into cherry mixture. For dumplings, in a small bowl, whisk flour, sugar, baking powder, lemon zest and salt. In another bowl, whisk milk and melted butter. Add to flour mixture; stir just until moistened. Drop by tablespoonfuls on top of hot cherry mixture. Cover with glass lid. Press slow cook function; select vegetables setting. Press timer; set to 1 hour. Start.

3. Remove glass lid; close air frying lid. Press air fry function; select bake setting. Press timer; set to 10 minutes. Start. Cook until lightly browned. If desired, serve warm with ice cream.

1 CUP: *398 cal., 6g fat (4g sat. fat), 16mg chol., 255mg sod., 78g carb. (55g sugars, 2g fiber), 4g pro.*

PEACH CRUMBLE

PREP: 30 MIN. | **SLOW-COOK:** 4 HRS. | **AIR-FRY:** 4 MIN. | **MAKES:** 8 SERVINGS

1 Tbsp. butter, softened

6 large ripe peaches, peeled and sliced (about 6 cups)

¼ cup all-purpose flour

2 Tbsp. light brown sugar

1 Tbsp. lemon juice

1 Tbsp. vanilla extract

2 Tbsp. coconut rum, optional

TOPPING

½ cup all-purpose flour

⅓ cup packed brown sugar

¾ tsp. baking powder

½ tsp. ground cinnamon

¼ tsp. baking soda

⅛ tsp. salt

½ cup old-fashioned oats

¼ cup butter, melted

1. Grease inner pot with 1 Tbsp. softened butter. Toss peaches with flour, brown sugar, lemon juice, vanilla and, if desired, rum; spread evenly in inner pot. Whisk together first 6 topping ingredients; stir in oats. Cut in butter until crumbly; sprinkle over peaches. Cover with glass lid. Press slow cook function; select vegetables setting. Press timer; set to 4 hours. Start.

2. Remove glass lid; close air frying lid. Press air fry function; select custom setting. Press timer; set to 4 minutes. Start. Cook until the topping is lightly browned. Serve warm.

¾ CUP: *237 cal., 8g fat (5g sat. fat), 19mg chol., 182mg sod., 39g carb. (25g sugars, 3g fiber), 3g pro.*

※ *Cobblers offer a biscuit or pastry topping placed over fruit for a cobblestone effect. Crumbles feature a cake-like streusel made of butter, flour and sugar sprinkled over fruit. Crisps are similar to crumbles, but their topping is crunchy and typically includes oats and nuts.*

APPLE PUDDING CRISP

PREP: 30 MIN. | **PRESSURE-COOK:** 25 MIN. + RELEASING | **AIR-FRY:** 7 MIN.
MAKES: 8 SERVINGS

6 **medium tart apples,
peeled and sliced**

1 **cup sugar**

¼ **cup all-purpose flour**

2 **tsp. ground cinnamon**

2 **large eggs**

1 **cup heavy whipping cream**

1 **tsp. vanilla extract**

TOPPING

½ **cup graham cracker crumbs**

⅓ **cup chopped pecans**

2 **Tbsp. butter, melted**

Vanilla ice cream, optional

1. Pour 1 cup water into inner pot. In a large bowl, combine apples, sugar, flour and cinnamon. Spoon into a greased 2-qt. round baking dish. In a small bowl, whisk eggs, cream and vanilla; pour over apple mixture.

2. Tightly cover dish with foil to prevent moisture from getting inside. Cut two 20x3-in. strips of heavy-duty foil; crisscross so they resemble an "X." Place dish in center of "X" shape; use strips as handles to lower dish onto rack in inner pot. Lock pressure lid. Press pressure function; select bake setting. Press timer; set to 25 minutes. Start.

3. Let pressure release naturally for 10 minutes, then quick-release any remaining pressure.

4. In a small bowl, combine cracker crumbs, pecans and butter; sprinkle over top. Cover with air frying lid. Press air fry function; select bake setting. Press timer; set to 7 minutes. Start. Cook until topping is lightly browned. Serve warm, with ice cream if desired.

1 SERVING: *365 cal., 19g fat (10g sat. fat), 88mg chol., 78mg sod., 47g carb. (38g sugars, 3g fiber), 4g pro.*

PEPPERMINT LAVA CAKES

PREP: 15 MIN. | **AIR-FRY:** 10 MIN. | **MAKES:** 4 SERVINGS

⅔ cup semisweet chocolate chips

½ cup butter, cubed

1 cup confectioners' sugar

2 large eggs

2 large egg yolks

1 tsp. peppermint extract

6 Tbsp. all-purpose flour

2 Tbsp. finely crushed peppermint candies, optional

1. In a microwave-safe bowl, melt chocolate chips and butter for 30 seconds; stir until smooth. Whisk in confectioners' sugar, eggs, egg yolks and extract until blended. Fold in flour.

2. Generously grease and flour four 4-oz. ramekins; pour batter into ramekins. Do not overfill. Place ramekins on wire basket with handles; carefully lower into inner pot. Close air frying lid. Press air fry function; select custom setting. Press timer; set to 10 minutes. Start. Cook until a thermometer reads 160° and edges of cakes are set, 10-12 minutes. Do not overcook.

3. Lift the rack from inner pot; let stand 5 minutes. Carefully run a knife around sides of ramekins several times to loosen cake; invert onto dessert plates. If desired, sprinkle with crushed candies. Serve immediately.

1 CAKE: *563 cal., 36g fat (21g sat. fat), 246mg chol., 226mg sod., 57g carb. (45g sugars, 2g fiber), 7g pro.*

Fast Yet Festive Garnish

1. To finely crush peppermint candy, put the candy in a resealable storage bag and crush with a rolling pin.

2. Continue crushing until candy pieces reach the desired size and texture.

FIG PEAR STRUDELS

PREP: 1 HOUR + STANDING | **AIR-FRY:** 6 MIN./BATCH + COOLING
MAKES: 4 STRUDELS (2 SLICES EACH)

2   medium pears, peeled
    and chopped

¼   cup pear nectar

2   Tbsp. brown sugar

1½ tsp. plus ½ cup
    butter, divided

½   tsp. grated lemon zest

⅛   tsp. ground allspice

    Dash salt

1½ tsp. cornstarch

1½ tsp. water

½   cup chopped dried figs

½   cup mascarpone cheese

1   Tbsp. heavy whipping
    cream

½   tsp. vanilla extract

16 sheets frozen phyllo dough,
    thawed (14x9-in. sheet size)

1   cup finely chopped
    black walnuts

2   Tbsp. coarse sugar

1. Combine pears, pear nectar, brown sugar, 1½ tsp. butter, lemon zest, allspice and salt in inner pot. Lock pressure lid. Press pressure function; select custom setting. Press timer; set to 1 minute. Start.

2. Quick-release pressure. Combine cornstarch and water until smooth. Gradually stir into pear mixture. Press saute function; select vegetables setting. Start. Bring to a boil; cook and stir 2 minutes or until thickened. Press cancel; stir in figs. Cover and let stand for 10 minutes.

3. In a small bowl, combine mascarpone cheese, cream and vanilla; set aside. Place 1 sheet of phyllo dough on a work surface; melt 7 Tbsp. remaining butter. Brush phyllo with melted butter. (Keep remaining phyllo covered with plastic wrap and a damp towel to prevent it from drying out.) Repeat with 2 more sheets of phyllo, brushing each layer with butter. Sprinkle with ¼ cup walnuts. Repeat. Top with 2 sheets of phyllo, brushing each layer with butter. Repeat with remaining phyllo, melted butter and walnuts. Cut each phyllo stack in half lengthwise.

4. Dollop cheese mixture by teaspoonfuls over phyllo to within ¼ in. of edges. Spread pear mixture over half of cheese mixture. Roll up jelly-roll style, starting with the short side spread with pear mixture. Wipe inner pot clean.

5. Place tall wire rack into inner pot. Arrange 2 strudels seam side down on greased rack. Melt remaining 1 Tbsp. butter. Using a sharp knife, cut slits in top. Brush with butter and sprinkle with coarse sugar. Cover with air frying lid. Press air fry function; select custom setting. Press timer; set to 6 minutes. Start. Cook until golden brown. Repeat with remaining 2 strudels. Cool to room temperature. Cut into slices.

1 SLICE: *482 cal., 36g fat (16g sat. fat), 70mg chol., 234mg sod., 37g carb. (18g sugars, 4g fiber), 9g pro.*

PARMESAN CRISP APPLES

PREP: 25 MIN. | **PRESSURE-COOK:** 8 MIN. + RELEASING | **AIR-FRY:** 7 MIN.
MAKES: 2 SERVINGS

2 medium Braeburn
   or Gala apples

3 Tbsp. grated
   Parmesan cheese

2 Tbsp. quick-cooking oats

2 Tbsp. all-purpose flour

4 tsp. packed brown sugar

   Dash ground nutmeg

1 Tbsp. butter, melted

   Honey, optional

1. Add 1 cup of water to the inner pot. Cut a ¼-in. slice off top of each apple. Core apples, leaving bottoms intact.

2. In a small bowl, mix cheese, oats, flour, brown sugar and nutmeg; stir in melted butter until crumbly. Carefully fill apples with oat mixture. Place stuffed apples in a baking dish (must fit inside inner pot) and cover tightly with foil. Place covered dish on wire rack with handles; use handles to lower into inner pot over water. Lock pressure lid. Press pressure function; select custom setting. Press timer; set to 8 minutes. Start.

3. Let pressure release naturally for 5 minutes, then quick-release any remaining pressure.

4. Remove foil. Close air frying lid. Press air fry function; select custom setting. Press timer; set to 7 minutes. Start. Cook until topping is lightly browned. To serve, drizzle with honey, if desired.

1 STUFFED APPLE: *242 cal., 9g fat (5g sat. fat), 22mg chol., 185mg sod., 40g carb. (25g sugars, 4g fiber), 4g pro.*

✳ *Braeburn and Gala apples are sweet, juicy and firm, making them ideal for this dessert. They can withstand heat without falling apart or becoming mushy, and they perfectly complement the homey filling.*

VERY VANILLA CHEESECAKE

PREP: 20 MIN. | **PRESSURE-COOK:** 65 MIN. + COOLING | **MAKES:** 6 SERVINGS

¾ cup graham cracker crumbs

1 Tbsp. plus ⅔ cup
sugar, divided

¼ tsp. ground cinnamon

2½ Tbsp. butter, melted

2 pkg. (8 oz. each) cream
cheese, softened

2 to 3 tsp. vanilla extract

2 large eggs, lightly beaten

TOPPING (OPTIONAL)

4 oz. semisweet baking
chocolate, chopped

2 tsp. vegetable shortening

Sliced almonds

1. Grease a 6-in. springform pan; pour 1 cup water into inner pot.

2. Mix cracker crumbs, 1 Tbsp. sugar and cinnamon; stir in butter. Press onto bottom and about 1 in. up sides of prepared springform pan.

3. In another bowl, beat cream cheese and remaining sugar until smooth. Beat in vanilla. Add eggs; beat on low speed just until combined. Pour over the crust.

4. Cover cheesecake tightly with foil. Place springform pan on wire rack with handles; lower into inner pot. Lock pressure lid. Press pressure function; select custom setting. Press timer; set to 65 minutes. Start. Cook until center of cheesecake is almost set.

5. Quick-release pressure. Remove springform pan from pressure cooker; remove foil. Cool cheesecake on a wire rack 1 hour. Loosen sides from pan with a knife. Refrigerate overnight, covering when completely cooled.

6. For topping, if desired, melt chocolate and shortening in a microwave; stir until smooth. Cool slightly. Remove rim from springform pan. Pour chocolate mixture over cheesecake. Sprinkle with almonds to serve.

1 SLICE: *484 cal., 34g fat (19g sat. fat), 151mg chol., 357mg sod., 39g carb. (31g sugars, 0 fiber), 8g pro.*

INDEX *General*

INDEX *Alphabetical*